Tips & Tactics for

Using the Internet to Run Your Business

by Greg Holden

Inc. Business Resources
Boston, Massachusetts

Published by *Inc.* Business Resources,
a division of Gruner + Jahr USA Publishing,
publisher of *Inc.* magazine.
Copyright © 2000 by Gruner + Jahr USA Publishing,
Boston, MA
All rights reserved.

No part of this book may be used or reproduced
in any manner whatsoever without written permission
from the publisher. For information, please write:
Permissions Manager, *Inc.* Business Resources,
38 Commercial Wharf, Boston, MA 02110-3883.

Editorial Director: Bradford W. Ketchum, Jr.
Book Project Manager: Gail E. Anderson
Text Designer: Martha Abdella

This publication is designed to provide accurate and
authoritative information in regard to the subject matter
covered. However, the publisher is not engaged in rendering
legal, accounting, or other professional advice. If legal
advice or other expert assistance is required, the services
of a competent professional should be sought. Companies that
conduct operations on the Internet are evolving constantly,
as are URLs. While every effort has been made to ensure the
accuracy of information in this book, readers should be aware
that Web addresses are subject to change.

This book may be purchased in bulk at discounted rates for
sales promotions, premiums, or fund-raising. Custom books
and excerpts of this publication are available. Contact:
Custom Publishing Sales Dept.
Inc. Business Resources
38 Commercial Wharf
Boston, MA 02110-3883
(1-800-394-1746).

ISBN 1-58230-017-8

First Edition

Printed in the United States of America.

www.inc.com

Contents

Chapter 1   5
Using the Internet for Business
- What Internet technology can do...
- ...and what it can't do
- What "B2B" means
- Is your business right for the Net?

Chapter 2   12
In-house Systems
- Why set up an intranet?
- Client/server technology
- Deploying software, sharing data
- Who gets access?
- Content and usage policies
- Getting employees to use the intranet
- Corporate portals
- Bandwidth: How much do you need?

Chapter 3   25
Administrative Procedures
- Hardware and software requirements
- Application Service Providers (ASPs)
- Communicating essential information
- Net-based bookkeeping/payroll
- Outsourced HR services
- Online training

Chapter 4   35
Procurement & Inventory Management
- B2B supplier sites
- Posting RFQs online
- B2B auctions
- Finding new vendors
- Group purchasing
- Real-time inventory

Chapter 5   47
Partner Networks
- ABCs of extranets
- Security issues
- Virtual private networks (VPNs)
- Customizing content for outsiders

Contents

Chapter 6   **57**
Secure Private Connections
- Applications for secure VPNs
- VPN software
- Network integration
- Outsourcing a VPN

Chapter 7   **66**
Internet Security
- What have you got to lose?
- Developing a security policy
- User authentication
- Firewalls
- Proprietary networks
- Encryption

Chapter 8   **75**
Online Communities
- Why join a B2B community?
- Finding potential clients
- Bartering for goods and services
- Bulletin boards/discussion groups
- Chat and messaging
- Videoconferencing

Chapter 9   **87**
Keeping Up with Technology
- Thinking in Internet time
- Monitoring your systems
- Sources of technology news
- Personal networking

CyberSpeak   **93**
A glossary of terms for dealing with the Internet

Chapter 1

Using the Internet for Business

When Health Decisions, a clinical research and development company in Chapel Hill, N.C., opened an office in Oxford, England, it turned to the Internet to ease its growing pains. The newly enlarged staff uses e-mail to keep in touch, the Web to purchase travel accommodations, and the company *intranet* to read orientation information and get answers to its human resources questions. An intranet is an internal computer network that uses Internet technology, such as Web servers and browsers, to allow employees to access and share information. Thanks to new streamlined procedures, hiring additional administrative staff, in fact, has proved unnecessary for the company, even with more personnel to keep track of and increased travel needs. (See "Intranet Helps Company Stay Healthy," page 7.)

Health Decisions' applications illustrate just some of the ways you can run your small or midsize company on the Internet. Reducing paperwork, increasing effective communication, ordering supplies, and collaborating with other businesses by using the Internet are among the tips and tactics described in this book.

As a decision-maker for your company, you need to be aware of new technologies that can increase not only profits but also the efficiency of day-to-day operations. One of the most effective approaches for improving your bottom line is through Internet business-to-business (B2B) commerce, which is replacing business-to-consumer (B2C) transactions as the fastest growing area of Web commerce.

The strategies described in this book are ideal for small to midsize companies that already have Web sites and an in-house IT staff (or an existing association with an outside service provider). But even if your company is very small, you can still benefit by using the Internet.

What Internet technology can—and can't—do for you. For one thing, the Net saves time. The chart below shows the time it takes for Health Decisions to complete standard procedures supported by Internet technology compared with standard times for those same procedures reported by others in the pharmaceutical industry. If you already use the Internet to manage your company and reach out to other businesses, however, keep in mind that the Net can't do everything.

Health Decisions CEO Michael Rosenberg cautions: "Technology, including intranets, are only tools, and they will never take the place of careful judgment and thought. Use the Internet as a tool to help get rid of the less rewarding aspects of work, and focus on the more rewarding [ones]." In other words, don't depend on Internet B2B to handle traditional tasks such as:

INTERNET TIME VS. INDUSTRY STANDARD

METRIC	HEALTH DECISIONS	INDUSTRY STANDARD
Study start-up (months)	1.5	5
Questionnaire validation (days)	<1	30
Queries (per page)	0.05	1
Database error (per 10k fields)	10	50
Last patient-last questionnaire (days)	3	35
Last patient-database lock (days)	4	122
Time to first regulatory submission (months)	4	12
Time for three regulatory submissions (months)	4	20

Source: Health Decisions

- *Determining what constitutes a good deal*
- *Ensuring that vendors are reliable*
- *Preparing your staff for new technology and increased access to information*

What does "B2B" mean for your employees? When you link employees to one another and to other individuals around the world through the Internet, you dramatically alter the way they work. Be sure to discuss the following changes with them:

- *Increased access to information.* At The Motley Fool, an Alexandria, Va., financial investment site, networking has revolutionized the way the com-

---

INTRANET HELPS COMPANY STAY "HEALTHY"

Could you manage 46 full-time employees, some of whom work overseas, with only 1.5 administrative staff? It can be done: Health Decisions, a North Carolina clinical research and development company, gets by with only an accountant and one HR professional by posting its orientation information for new employees on its intranet. Staff can also purchase travel vouchers and record purchases made with company credit cards online.

Like many "wired" organizations, Health Decisions also publishes the company news online. Improved communication and workflow—thanks to e-mail, the intranet, and access to the wider Internet—enable critical procedures to be handled far more quickly than industry standards.

CEO Michael Rosenberg estimates that the company "would require five to seven additional people if we used conventional communications, at an average cost of $35K. This means our intranet is saving us about $175K to $245K per year."

pany's 350 employees interact with customers. The previous one-to-many model has given way to a many-to-many community atmosphere that increases customer loyalty—but also increases the burden on individual employees to make sure the information they share is accurate and valuable, and that it does not violate confidentiality.

• *A greater need for rules and standards.* When your employees have the ability to place their own supply orders, you soon may find them requesting such "necessities" as Dilbert mouse pads and MontBlanc pens. Control, tracking, and management oversight are essential. Look for sites (such as Works.com, which specializes in providing automated purchasing solutions for businesses over the Internet) that will forward orders to your in-house purchasing agent for approval or that allow you to set up a list of approved items for purchase.

Internet suitability. You're not going to jump on the Net just because everyone else is doing it. But there are ways of knowing whether or not you should make the move. The Internet is right for your business if:

• *You need to save money.* EnSafe, an environmental and safety services provider in Memphis, hasn't had to increase its prices significantly for the past five years; as employees become more productive, the company is able to accomplish more with fewer individuals. Employees log their activities and prioritize assignments using their individual networked computers. They communicate by e-mail; team goals and financial data are posted on the company's internal network; and reports (which formerly were multivolume treatises) are delivered electronically. EnSafe's overhead has been steadily declining, thanks to Internet B2B.

• *You need to communicate better internally.* Adopting Internet-based client/server technology enables EnSafe's employees to communicate in ways with which they are already familiar. They can exchange e-mail, communicate in real time—using chat or conferencing software—or post messages on company bulletin boards.

• *You need to communicate with other businesses instantly.* Internet technology makes sense if your company needs to exchange mission-critical information with other businesses in a matter of minutes, if not seconds. In 1998, EnSafe used a secure password-protected part of its company intranet, called an extranet, to post digital photos of an emergency involving toxic gas cylinders. Industry experts and clients could track what was happening and make decisions as events unfolded.

• *You need to collaborate (and cut back on travel and telecommunication expenses).* If you and your business colleagues who work in different locations need to share images to develop projects or do collaborative problem solving, the Internet gives you a variety of options. You don't have to use expensive conferencing centers or set up leased lines in order to conduct virtual meetings. You can post images on Web pages; use conferencing software, such as Windows NetMeeting by Microsoft, to work online with whiteboards; or use Internet phone technology to make otherwise expensive long-distance phone calls through your computer. While the sound quality of voice transmission in Internet phone technology can leave something to be desired, watch for further innovations in this rapidly developing field.

> **TIP** The Internet gives employees even less of an excuse not to share data and work in a collaborative fashion. Not only can staff communicate by e-mail, but they also can publish data in the form of Web pages that can be browsed on the intranet. The Motley Fool lets its employees "talk" on its intranet by means of message boards and surveys. The Internet gives you, as manager, new tools for getting the various parts of your company to work together.

> **TIP** You don't need to invest significant capital to benefit from online B2B. Smaller organizations can cut their investment and costs substantially by joining vertical trade communities on the Internet. These are groups of businesses that meet online to exchange goods and services in a particular field, such as the 14 business communities—or industries—hosted by VerticalNet.

- *You need to expand your supplier/customer base.* Internet communication technologies such as Web pages, e-mail, bulletin boards, videoconferencing, and chat can help you find new business partners. iPrint.com, the leading online print shop and print infrastructure provider with nearly 200 employees in Redwood City, Calif., finds the majority of its customers through its Web site, and nearly all of its printing work uses some form of Internet hardware or software. Besides enabling customers to place print orders over the Web, iPrint also helps other businesses set up their own online print shops running on iPrint.com technology, which adds significantly to the company's customer base.
- *You need to make it easy for business colleagues to find you.* Your business does not have to be new or even high tech in nature to benefit from Internet B2B. Pepper Construction, a 73-year-old Barrington, Ill., company that builds office complexes, renovates museums, and undertakes other nonresidential construction projects, has leveraged its Web-based communications. Pepper employees can keep track of the company's inventory of building materials more quickly than in the past by accessing a shared intranet database and can place orders online closer to the time the particular building stock is needed—within one week, in some cases. Although the company

does not have a public URL, its sales have shot up more than 900% in the last three years, thanks in part to better Web-based communication.

• *You want to break down trade barriers.* The ability to share data and communicate quickly using the Internet enables companies to reach new markets overseas. You can locate trade publications that provide business users in a particular industry—such as energy, healthcare, or high technology—with online bulletin boards or classified advertising sections.

• *You need to cut administrative overhead.* The Internet can also help you slash day-to-day operating costs. At The Motley Fool, back-end management tools that include such basics as inventory control, billing, and employee-feedback programs have given the company the ability to perform work that would otherwise require a staff four or five times larger. At EnSafe, everyone uses a networked computer to log activities and prioritize assignments—even the janitor has a workstation at his desk.

It is only common sense that you can manage your business better when you are able to share data efficiently. When clean and accurate data is delivered efficiently, the implications for your enterprise can be significant. ∎

COMPANIES AND SITES IN THIS CHAPTER

EnSafe **www.ensafe.com**
Health Decisions **www.healthdec.com**
iPrint.com **www.iprint.com**
Microsoft **www.microsoft.com**
The Motley Fool **www.fool.com**
VerticalNet **www.verticalnet.com**
Works.com **www.works.com**

Chapter 2

In-house Systems

B2B doesn't just mean doing business with other companies or providing access to your company to individuals outside your organization. It also refers to techniques that enable the various segments of one company to communicate with one another. You might see these referred to as business-to-employee (B2E) communications.

An internal network that uses Internet technology to manage information within an organization is called an intranet. If you need to enable your staff to share ideas or if you need to connect employees who work in far-flung locations, establishing an intranet is a logical first step.

Why set up an intranet? Why should you consider changing to an intranet that uses funny-sounding Internet protocols like TCP/IP and HTTP when an in-house local area network (LAN) may already be enabling your employees to share information through software such as Lotus Notes?

Because an intranet is Web-based, there are two big pluses: employees' familiarity with Web browsers and the ability to click on hyperlinks. An intranet makes the connection between a company's internal network and the external Internet truly seamless because your staff already knows how to use the Internet.

Also, by switching to an intranet, you can minimize hardware-incompatibility issues and software-driver problems. Rather than using a proprietary networking program to serve and share files, you install a Web server that is platform independent. Netscape Enterprise Server is a popular choice for server software; Netscape Communicator or Microsoft Internet Explorer can be deployed as client programs.

Internet software makes it very easy to access internal networks remotely. You don't need to know special access numbers or to set up modem protocols. You connect to the Net the way you always do, then enter the URL for your company Web site in your browser and press "Return."

Of course, you will need to set up a security system that requires a user to enter an approved user name and password, so that users can view intranet pages (see Chapter 7). A firewall or other hardware security program, such as eSafe Gateway by Aladdin Knowledge Systems, can provide a practical solution for small and midsize companies.

The Advanced Group of Cos., a staffing firm based in Deerfield, Ill., that provides temporary and direct-hire employees as well as consultants to companies nationwide, uses its internal network and the Internet to link 14 offices with more than 180 employees in six states. The company uses a feature called high-bandwidth frame relay that enables businesses to obtain high-speed Internet access at an affordable price (see "Reach Out and Touch Everyone," on page 20). The Advanced Group's "Partner on Premise" program enables a client to notify the company of its staffing requirements via the Web. The order is reviewed immediately and then submitted online to The Advanced Group's staffing partners.

Another application—processing paycheck information on the Internet and intranet—increases accounting efficiency and reduces errors for The Advanced Group. The company expects revenues to grow to $200 million in the next two years, due in part to its technology initiatives.

Client/server technology. Intranets run on the same sort of client/server technology on which the Internet itself is built. What are some of the things that make intranets different and that you will need to discuss with your IT staff? Here are some suggestions:

• *Web authoring.* Documents made available on an intranet are essentially Web documents. The bulk of intranet content consists of Web pages with images, hyperlinks, and other familiar elements. Will you need to hire someone to convert your important internal content to Web-page, or HTML, format? Not necessarily. Some Web-authoring programs, such as Adobe PageMill® or the powerful Macromedia Dreamweaver 3.0, are available to enable even tech-challenged staff to create the pages themselves. Get your more technically minded staff to help the others.

• *E-mail.* You may already have an e-mail system. However, if you want e-mail that is integrated with the Web browsers that will be used to access files, consider switching to an Internet-based post office protocol (POP3) e-mail server, such as Eudora WorldMail Server, by QUALCOMM.

• *Subdomains.* You probably already have a Web site that uses your corporate domain—www.company.com, for instance. You can readily divide important areas of your intranet into easy-to-find addresses such as home.company.com, news.company.com, and so on.

• *Downsizing fears.* When hiring information, personnel documents, time-reporting forms, and the like are placed online, some employees (such as HR personnel) may fear they will become unnecessary. Allay their fears by explaining that the use of an intranet is part of your company's evolution and not meant to put anyone out of a job.

Web browsers: a uniform interface to information. Web browsers let you access networked information from virtually any computer in any location. You don't have to have spreadsheet software to view accounting information or a scheduling program to schedule upcoming meetings, for example. The upshot: You and your employees should get used to being able to access data on a 24/7 basis, without having to ask certain staff to retrieve information and generate reports before they can be reviewed.

Web sites are springing up all the time, and you'll need software that will enable you to access all potential marketplaces. The Web browser will do

TIP If your employees frequently work in other offices on a consulting basis, consider providing them with a Web-browser-based interface to check their e-mail. This allows them to send and receive e-mail without having to obtain an account from the company at which they are working. (Some client offices might have security systems called firewalls that make it difficult for your employees to send and receive e-mail using the client's program.) Your employees would use their Web browser to manage their mail in much the same way that someone uses Hotmail, the popular free e-mail service.

this on the front end, enabling suppliers to make inventory available and procurers to access products and place orders.

In order to make transactions viable among companies and systems that do not usually communicate with one another, software on the companies' respective back ends needs to be integrated as well. You may need an application integration platform such as e*Xchange™ Integrator, by Software Technologies Corp. Such software translates data so it can be understood by the platforms used by all participating companies.

Developing your intranet. You don't need to flood your intranet with all of your company information at the same time. Put selected data online in stages. While the new system is being developed, it can coexist with your existing network.

Like many company managers, you may have a substantial amount of internal documentation to put online, while your staff may be anxious to browse other material—company news, personal home pages, scheduling calendars, classified ads, and photos from the last company party. If your staff people express an interest in creating their own intranet content, appoint a review board that will determine what will go on the intranet. The board can ensure that the critical information you want employees to share will appear there, as well as the social content that makes using an intranet enjoyable.

Determining who gets access. Begin by determining how much of your operation will need to be covered by your intranet. You might ask your colleagues the following sorts of questions:

• *Do you want to put your company policies and procedures and insurance information online?*

• *Do you want to create special Web pages called "bulletin boards" on which individuals can post social messages?*

• *Do you want to post earnings reports, expense-account forms, and other accounting information?*

• *Will you be sharing purchase-order and payroll information?*

• *Will you post job openings and the company newsletter?*

Make a list of all the tasks you want to be able to handle on the intranet and prioritize which ones need to be tackled first.

When you are devising the architecture for your intranet, make a list of the people (e.g., business partners, prospective employees) who might need to access specialized information that you don't want the entire world to see. For those parties, you can set up an extranet: a protected area of your intranet that only particular external users can access.

Deploying software and sharing data. What sort of information would you want to access on an intranet? Anderson & Associates, a professional engineering and design services firm based in Blacksburg, Va., provides a wealth of information on its corporate intranet, including:

• *Procedures to follow when publishing bid information*

• *Downloadable software, with general information about the programs*

• The Scoop, *the company's employee newsletter*

• *Employee manuals*

- *Information on the employee stock ownership plan*
- *"A&A Faces" page, featuring information about individual employees*

Who creates content? Since most intranet content is in the form of Web pages, your company's printed and electronic documents need to be in Web-page format. If they are not, you'll need to convert them. This can be a time-consuming process if you have a substantial amount of content to translate. You can hire a Webmaster full-time to create and manage your intranet content, but such an individual typically commands a salary in the $80,000 to $100,000 range. Fortunately, there are alternatives.

Pinnacle Decision Systems, a professional services and software development company based in Middletown, Conn., spent only $9,000 to $10,000 to develop its intranet, but that's partly because its in-house staff created it. The cost to contract out the networking and software installation could range from tens of thousands to hundreds of thousands of dollars, depending on the range of sophistication you need. Pinnacle has adapted its own intranet as a commercial product called HQ Intranet, which it sells for about $20,000. Pinnacle COO John Mulvaney advises businesses that are planning their own intranets to "start small, and put your information on the network gradually." (For more details on how Pinnacle leverages its intranet, see, "Reach Out and Touch

TIP Where do you come up with interesting, useful content that will entice employees to use your intranet on a daily basis? Consider contracting with a syndication service such as isyndicate.com, which offers subscriptions to news feeds from nearly 1,000 sources, ranging from The Associated Press and *Business Week* to AccuWeather and industry-specific business services.

> **TIP** Need to create Web content from spreadsheet programs or word processors? Look to Microsoft Office 2000, whose component programs (Word, Excel, and Outlook PowerPoint) can export files to HTML format (hypertext markup language—the formatting language used to create Web pages) with a single menu command. While it's not always a perfect export, it's worth trying this short cut.

Everyone," on page 20.)

Programs such as Microsoft FrontPage are powerful Web-authoring tools that enable employees to format text for their own Web pages, as well as add images, hyperlinks, and other content. Some training, as well as design expertise, is required.

On the other hand, you may decide that personal Web pages should be kept off the intranet. Establish clear usage policies. An employee directory with photos and contact information for each person can be useful for suppliers and business partners who need to find a particular staff member. Bulletin boards, discussion groups, and e-mail provide many more ways for employees to interact than traditional watercooler encounters or staff meetings. They're also a means of posting clearly spelled-out rules that employees can refer to about what constitutes the proper use of computer resources on the job—and what constitutes misuse.

Intranet publishing priorities. You can accomplish such a wide variety of tasks with an intranet that the problem becomes one of prioritizing those uses. Determine which goals are most important for your company and address them on your intranet.

At GNP Computers, a computer and telecommunications solutions company based in Monrovia, Calif., the goals were increasing sales, improving

> **TIP** A directory service, or "White Pages" area that contains contact information about each person in the company, is an important part of many corporate intranets. Thanks to Internet technology, the directory can be made searchable. For instance, if you don't remember someone's first or last name or an exact spelling, you can search for the person using the part of his or her name that you do remember. Such a directory is commonly created using a special Internet set of standard instructions called Lightweight Directory Access Protocol (LDAP).

employee morale, and providing better customer service. GNP has lifted morale by giving its 140 employees recognition for superior sales performance, plus access to a "virtual store" and a company-events page on its intranet. Staff can also access benefits information on 401(k) plans and health care, including links to their benefits providers' Web sites. The sense of community that develops as a result of shared access to data and communications paths is especially valuable for employees of smaller organizations.

Encourage employees to use your intranet. While there's nothing wrong with posting benefits options or phone directories online, consider these tips for spicing up an intranet to entice employees to use it regularly:

• *Make it attractive.* Make your employee intranet just as inviting and well-organized as your external, public Web site.

• *Let employees contribute.* If you have programmers to create Web-page forms and other systems for your external site, you easily could have them create a form with which individuals or workgroups could create their own Web pages. As long as the content isn't offensive (or for profit), it's a good way to give people a feeling that they have a personal stake in the intranet.

• *Keep it fresh.* Assign someone to frequently update your intranet. Make it the place to go for company news.

• *Publish material that people will want to know about.* Employees need to know meeting schedules, but they also want the scoop on the stock-ownership program, revenues, or where and when the next outing will be held.

Should you create a corporate portal? A growing trend among businesses that conduct Internet B2B is the creation of a Web page that provides a single entry point—a portal—to the company's information. Such a page contains a brief description of the business, plus links to the main areas of its Web site. A portal such as the well-known Yahoo! home page tries to attract

---

REACH OUT AND TOUCH EVERYONE

Access to information—and to their coworkers—has always been key for the staff of Pinnacle Decision Systems. Pinnacle's 50 full-time employees work as consultants, developing software for client companies in at least five Northeastern states.

"Before we set up our intranet and e-mail access," says COO John Mulvaney, "people working in other regions had no idea what was going on in the company. Our employees might not see each other for weeks or months at a time."

Pinnacle's intranet not only facilitates communication but also helps convey the company's open-book management style, which allows employees to track how well the company is doing through its intranet.

"The level of detail to which employees have access makes them aware of more than just their personal goals," says Mulvaney. "It encourages them to identify with the needs of our customers. That, of course, has to be bal-

the widest number of users from across the Internet. It contains links to different services provided by Yahoo!, as well as an index by category of links to every conceivable topic.

A vertical portal, or vortal, serves the same function as a portal but focuses on a single topic. The vortal directs users with a single interest to online information in that field. A good example of a vortal is the home page of The Motley Fool's Web site, which contains many entry points to the company's information for financial investors and to selected locations around the Internet that are related to subjects such as retirement and stock trading. eLabor.com, a labor resource planning solutions company with nearly 200

> anced with the overall goals of the company."
>
> Another advantage of an intranet is that it enables one voice to communicate with everyone in the company. A special e-mail address lets employees broadcast messages companywide.
>
> Pinnacle also uses its intranet to help draw prospective employees into the company. Before they start work, new hires receive a special password that gives them restricted access to the intranet's main pages.
>
> Another aspect of the Pinnacle intranet is Maven, an employee-led quality circle. Five staff people volunteer to serve as mavens and initiate new personnel procedures and organize social events. The minutes of the Maven group meetings are published on the intranet.
>
> Mulvaney says that because his employees are professionals, they don't abuse the ability to communicate so easily. What employees publish online should be subject to review, however. Pinnacle publishes a set of guidelines on the proper use of company computer resources. It also reminds staff that it monitors electronic traffic.

In-house Systems

> **TIP** The same technical specialists who created your existing Web site can put together an interactive portal. You also can use software especially designed to create portals, such as XPS, developed by Sequoia Software Corp.

employees based in Camarillo, Calif., provides a Workforce Portal of a community of "virtual employees" to its clients.

eLabor.com also communicates electronically with media, partners, and customers through its own specialized news service, which provides links not only to press releases but also to trade shows and other events in which eLabor.com will be participating. It also provides links to other labor and human resources sites on the Web.

Bandwidth. For many companies, the greater the data capacity (bandwidth) of the lines that connect local computers to one another and to the Internet, the faster business gets done. Bandwidth is most commonly measured in kilobits per second (Kbps) or megabits per second (Mbps). There are two types of bandwidth:

• *Internal.* Most often, LANs use a data transmission protocol called Ethernet to move data from one node (a computer, printer, or other device) to another on the network. Until recently, Ethernet came in two varieties. The "slow" type had a bandwidth of 10Mbps. Fast Ethernet, on the other hand, worked at 100Mbps. Now there's also Gigabit Ethernet, which has a one-gigabit capacity (1Gbps, or 1,000 Mbps).

How much bandwidth do you need? Gigabit Ethernet makes sense if: 1. Your company is built around the Internet, and data communications are central to your operation; 2. You commonly need to share complex graphics files, charts, and presentations; or 3. You plan to do a lot of videoconferencing. Otherwise, Fast Ethernet is adequate for most small and midsize businesses.

• *External.* The other type of bandwidth is the data-transfer capacity of the line that connects your company's computers to the external Internet. A dial-up modem connection that has a bandwidth of only 56Kbps is impractical for any but the smallest companies.

Conventional analog modems used with a conventional phone line are fine for individuals. But even small companies need direct, "always on" connections. If your company is small and on a tight budget, compare the following connection options:

- *T1*. A digital connection that uses the T-carrier system and is widely used among Internet service providers. It has a maximum data transfer speed of 1.544 Mbps.
- *Fractional T1*. A single T1 cable divided into 24 separate channels. A fractional T1 is some portion of those 24 channels leased to a customer to provide a connection that is less expensive than a full T1 line.
- *T3*. A souped-up version of the T1, with a bandwidth of 44.736 Mbps.
- *Frame relay*. A technology that enables multiple businesses to share a single high-speed line, such as a T1 or T3 line.
- *Asynchronous transfer mode (ATM)* A switching technology used to provide super-high-speed direct connections—up to 10 Gbps in some cases.
- *Cable modem*. A device that connects to the Internet through the same

> **TIP** If it seems to take a long time to copy files from the server to your computer on your local network, it might not be an Ethernet problem: Your server might have inadequate random access memory (RAM)—the memory used to run applications and copy data. (Servers running Windows 2000 need a bare minimum of 64MB of RAM, and work better with 96MB, 128MB, or more.)

type of wires used for cable TV. Cable modems have the capacity to deliver 4 to 5 Mbps of data, but it is shared with other users, so in reality, the speed is slower.

• *Digital subscriber line (DSL).* A digital Internet connection using conventional phone lines. This connection can send data at up to 1.088 Mbps and receive data at 2.560 Mbps. The catch is that you have to live near a DSL-supported switching station to be able to use this service.

Cable modem and DSL connections are relatively inexpensive options (less than $50 per month, plus installation fees) that provide you with an always-on connection and high bandwidth. Be sure to ask your provider if multiple computers can share the same connection; if they can, you'll need to install a router so all your employees can benefit from direct access. Check with your local cable or telephone supplier, or with national DSL suppliers to see if they serve your area. ■

COMPANIES AND SITES IN THIS CHAPTER

Adobe Systems www.adobe.com
Aladdin Knowledge Systems www.ealaddin.com
Anderson & Associates www.andassoc.com/index.html
eLabor.com www.elabor.com
GNP Computers www.gnp.com
Hotmail www.hotmail.com
iPrint.com www.iprint.com
iSyndicate www.isyndicate.com

Macromedia www.macromedia.com
Microsoft www.microsoft.com
Netscape www.netscape.com
QUALCOMM www.qualcomm.com
Sequoia Software www.sequoiasw.com
Software Technologies www.stc.com
The Motley Fool www.fool.com
Yahoo! www.yahoo.com

Chapter 3

Administrative Procedures

Orientation, one of the most important and potentially nerve-wracking experiences for new employees at any company, is now a less stressful and more rewarding process for new staff at Pinnacle Decision Systems, thanks to the Internet. Before new hires even begin their first day at the 14-year-old consulting and software-development firm based in Middletown, Conn., they get to meet coworkers and become a part of the team. They are eased into the corporate culture on their own terms—and in the comfort of their own homes—by connecting to the following resources:

• *The company intranet.* Pinnacle's intranet has its own Web address: http://hq.pinndec.com. (This URL is distinct from that of the company's external Web site, http://www.pinndec.com.) The intranet runs like a miniature version of the World Wide Web: Files are made available by Web servers and accessed by Web browsers and software that uses the Internet data transfer method called file transfer protocol, or FTP. New employees connect to the Net, start their Web browsers, and type in the intranet's URL. They then type in a user name and password to gain access to company information.

• *E-mail.* New employees are given the chance to select their own e-mail addresses. Once they have one, they can receive announcements that are distributed to all employees by an internal mailing list. They can also begin to exchange individual e-mail messages with their supervisors and coworkers.

• *Online discussion groups.* A discussion group is a way of connecting multiple Internet users so they can exchange messages on a given topic. At Pinnacle, groups on bulletin boards discuss matters as trivial as the sale of golf clubs or as weighty as new-product ideas. New employees can join in on gossip as well as ongoing project discussions and become part of the team right away.

> **TIP** An intranet requires a substantial commitment in time, personnel, and technology. You should allow at least six months to a year for this process and expect to hire a Webmaster, either on contract or full-time, to set up the system for you. An entire intranet system, including computers, networking equipment, and personnel, can cost from $10,000 to $100,000, depending on the size of the business.

On Pinnacle's intranet, employees can also communicate ideas for new sales strategies directly to higher management by filling out a Web-page form. The form contains text boxes, radio buttons, and check boxes to capture user-entry data and submit it to an e-mail address or a file on the central Web server. "We've gotten 15 to 20 ideas from the online form, which is quite a lot," says Pinnacle's director of information technology Stacey Kivel. "Before the Web, people wouldn't know where to go with their ideas. I think that sometimes it's intimidating to call someone with an idea."

Hardware requirements. The heart of an intranet is a Web server—a computer with a fast processor (at least 400MHz) and at least 128MB or more of RAM—as well as 5GB to 10GB of disk storage space. A given intranet may require the processing power of more than one Web server, depending on the size of the company.

You'll also need an e-mail server, a computer that acts as the routing point for incoming and outgoing mail. The e-mail server is equipped with software such as Microsoft Exchange Server, which uses both the Internet communications scheme Post Office Protocol (POP3) to route incoming messages to the correct recipients and simple mail transfer protocol to make sure outgoing mail is sent correctly.

To transfer information, you'll need a network of cables that run from computer to computer and use Ethernet, a data transmission protocol that enables computers to move data at speeds of 100Mbps or faster.

Software requirements. A Web server uses software to make files available to employees equipped with Web browsers. Freeware programs, such as Apache and Linux, can function as Web servers, as well as Microsoft's Internet Information Server.

Each computer on the network needs to be set up with software applications that act as the client in the client/server intranet system—which will retrieve files and present information to individual users. The most important client program is a Web browser, such as Microsoft Internet Explorer or Netscape Communicator (both of which are free). A copy of one of these programs should be distributed to all employees on the system, along with any FTP or discussion-group software you want employees to have.

After the system's infrastructure is set up, the Webmaster needs to create an internal Web site. A program such as Macromedia Dreamweaver 3.0 or Microsoft FrontPage 2000 is a good choice for "spinning" an integrated set of Web pages into a site that employees will want to turn to each day for company news and communications.

Application service providers (ASPs). An ASP is a Web-based service that provides software functionality that clients access online. Rather than purchasing and installing your own applications, you can connect to an ASP's site and make use of the software there. ASPs not only save you the trouble of installing and upgrading software on your own, but they also make your intranet and external Web site more functional, providing such highly technical features as:

- *Animated Web-page images.* An ASP such as Animation Technologies can handle this for you.

- *Real-time chat discussions.* Check out Digi-Net Technologies.
- *Videoconferences or audio conferences.* WebEx arranges these types of Internet-enabled meetings for businesses.

Journyx, a business software developer based in Austin, Tex., functions as an ASP by offering its own timesheet and expense-account applications online. The company's timesheet entry form includes a link to a start/stop timer feature that employees can use to track how much time they spend on a particular project. Journyx also provides its software to other ASPs so they, in turn, can offer them online to businesses. The company, which has fewer than 50 full-time employees, estimates that it is responsible for 70% of the Web-based timesheet/time-reporting market, and that 5,000 subscribers have signed up to use its services.

A good source for finding ASPs is internet.com's ASPnews.com, a Web site that functions as a clearinghouse for this relatively new industry. A caveat of using an ASP is that you are depending on provider-supplied technology. If the ASP's site or your Internet connection is down, you can't use the ASP's application.

Empower your employees. Once your intranet is in place, the next step is to set goals for its use. One of the initial goals to keep in mind is making employees feel more involved and empowered. Another is communicating policies and strategies to those employees. Make a list of all the "official" documents you can put online, such as employee handbooks, rules sheets, benefits packages, travel vouchers, and expense reports. Then think of ways you would like to see employees communicate and work more effectively.

Consider the example of Direct Partners, a one-to-one direct- and database-marketing company in Marina del Rey, Calif. This moderately sized organization (with a few hundred full-time employees) set out to become the largest direct-marketing agency on the West Coast. It achieved that goal by using the Internet to help reduce overhead by 30% as well as boost its profit margin. Here's how Direct Partners did it:

- *Book travel online.* Employees are allowed to book their own travel using Web-based travel services.
- *Order supplies online.* Office supplies, from pencils to computers, are purchased directly from business suppliers' online catalogs. (To ensure the proper use of electronic procurement, set up accounts with Internet-based catalog-supply houses that prevent orders from going through without the approval of designated managers.)
- *Make fewer in-person visits.* Individual staff members were able to reduce the number of trips they had to make by using online rate calculators, lists of drop-off locations, and shipping labels they downloaded from the Web sites of major shipping companies.
- *Transmit electronically.* Artwork, copy, television rough-cuts, etc., are transmitted electronically.

Communicate essential information. Pepper Construction handles large-scale building projects and renovations from its home office in Barrington, Ill. Its crews work long-term at job sites throughout the country. Although the company has no public URL, employees connect to the company's internal Web site to share job information and receive instructions from home base. The kind of companywide information that businesses such as Pepper can communicate to employees on the Web and through e-mail includes staff directories, policy handbooks, organizational charts, and answers to frequently asked questions.

Dan Caulfield, founder and CEO of Hire Quality, a Chicago-based company with 25 employees in three offices, turned his business's fortunes around when he decided to concentrate on managing information instead of people. Part of his strategy was opening up the company's books. Giving everyone access to revenue and other financial information over the company intranet gave employees better decision-making capabilities, he says.

Paperless time reporting. Expense-account reporting, timesheet recording, and the tracking of billable time can be expedited with the help of intranet Web pages and special time-management software. The same sorts of Webpage forms that your customers fill out to make purchases or register for services on your external Web site can be created for employees who need to record these daily activities on your internal database.

MapQuest.com (acquired by America Online in June 2000), a Manhattan-based online provider of mapping and destination information, has leveraged the Internet for its everyday functions. Until a couple of years ago, MapQuest was saddled with an antiquated MS-DOS-based accounting system. Whenever project-costing reports or month-end calculations were needed, a programmer had to be called in—at $150 per hour—to generate them.

MapQuest.com's solution: Use Microsoft Internet Information Server to create an intranet and connect the company to the Internet. MapQuest.com also used a

> **TIP** Open-book-management policies are popular, and they are more practical with the use of an intranet. But what does it take to implement open book online? You can install a tax-preparation package that connects to relevant Web sites, such as Money 2000 by Microsoft. Those software packages would have to be installed on the computer of each user who would require access to your books over the intranet. In a true open-book environment, you probably would need to purchase a multi-user license and distribute the software to everyone on your intranet.

EXTRA BENEFITS FROM AN EXTRANET

Pay Plus Benefits describes itself as a professional employer. The Kennewick, Wash., company sets up retirement and benefit plans and issues paychecks for its clients' employees. When a client contracts to use Pay Plus's services, the company receives its own miniature human resources Web site, which, in reality, is an extranet that resides on Pay Plus Benefits' own intranet. The client's employees can turn to the Web site 24 hours a day to check holiday schedules, do enrollment, download W2 forms, and perform other HR functions.

"Our service gives companies the ability to do better record-keeping. That puts a premium on accurate data entry when employees are initially entered into the system," says Pay Plus CEO John Heaton.

Pay Plus uses an intranet to share client information internally. And the company uses e-mail and scheduling software to keep its own 10 full-time employees informed of daily activities. Last year, the company's revenues jumped to $26 million. By leveraging Internet technology, Pay Plus was able to realize that level of growth with the addition of only a couple of technical staff and without having to expand its bricks-and-mortar facilities.

Administrative

project-accounting software package, Intellisol Project Accounting with Xpede, which enables its 160 employees to enter timesheet information using their Web browsers. Weekly internal reports can also be exported quickly to the popular spreadsheet program Microsoft Excel, then distributed through e-mail, giving managers the chance to analyze projects in near real-time.

After one month of using its new system, MapQuest.com cut in half the amount of work involved in generating month-end reports. The company now uses a weekly paperless report-distribution process, and employees enter their time on the Internet or the corporate network—a process that previously required as many as five hours of data entry per week.

An intranet, equipped with the right software, will allow your employees to record their billable hours and other work-related activities by filling out a Web-page form and submitting the data to a central server. You can easily track how much time your employees have spent on specific projects, too. This is one of the great advantages of the Internet: Electronically networked information is available and can be updated anytime, day or night.

Outsourced HR services. At AquaPrix, a Hayward, Calif., company that distributes water purification systems, "We are always looking for ways to stretch every dollar," said president/CEO Lynne Leahy. That's why she has turned to the Internet for office-support services, such as payroll and banking. "Online means it's done instantly," she says.

> **TIP** Consider enrolling your staff in distance learning courses, especially if you have only one or two individual employees who need to learn a specialized subject, such as Web-server or database management, and courses aren't offered in your immediate area. If a large number of employees need to sign up for the same course on a more basic subject (such as Microsoft Word or Excel 2000) and they can't all be out of the office at the same time, Web-based learning might be an effective route. Taking a course on the Web enables employees to learn at their own pace, on their own schedules.

If hiring, training, administering benefits, and other responsibilities are straining your accounting or human resources staff, you could hire an outside firm to handle your company's payroll needs. A growing number of companies, such as PayMaxx, in Franklin, Tenn., provide an Internet-enabled payroll system.

Other options include professional employer organizations (PEOs), which handle payroll and human resources functions for businesses on a contract basis. You'll find lists of PEOs at the Web sites for the Institute for the Accreditation of Professional Employer Organizations and the National Association of Professional Employer Organizations.

Outsourcing doesn't mean you are free of responsibility. Because PEOs work with sensitive personnel information, you have to research the providers thoroughly by interviewing them, checking their accreditation, and talking to other customers. Outsourcing makes sense for businesses that have employees or branches located in two or more places. And if your technical staff are too busy running your public Web site, you can hire a company such as Pay Plus Benefits to set up a customized Web site that your employees can access in order to view benefits and other information.

Online training. Before you arrange to send staff members to training seminars in remote locations or hire instructors to conduct classes in-house, look into the wealth of training opportunities already on the Web. (Better yet, suggest that prospective students on your staff explore the Web and report on online courses that seem relevant to their needs. Make sure they report on costs as well as any prerequisites they'll need before you have them enroll.) Here are a couple of the offerings:

• *Advanced courses.* DigitalThink provides advanced-level courses in network administration, desktop publishing, and many other topics. Its interactive courses come complete with tutors, graded exercises, and the ability to hold discussions with fellow students.

• *Courses for credit.* Some colleges and universities allow students to attend virtual classes for credit. Caroline Smith, 27, who works as a researcher in the pharmaceutical industry, in Research Triangle Park, N.C., got a head start on a PharmD. by enrolling in a microeconomics course at the University of North Carolina that combined televised and Web-based content. She entered an actual classroom only when it was time to take exams. ∎

COMPANIES AND SITES IN THIS CHAPTER

Animation Technologies **www.animationtechnologies.com**

Apache Software Foundation **www.apache.com**

Aquaprix **www.aquaprix.com**

Digi-Net Technologies **web.digi-net.com**

DigitalThink **www.digitalthink.com**

Direct Partners **www.directpartners.com**

Health Decisions **www.healthdec.com**

Hire Quality **www.hire-quality.com**

Institute for Accreditation of Professional Employer Organizations **www.iapeo.org**

Intellisol International **www.intellisol.com**

internet.com **www.aspnews.com**

Journyx **www.journyx.com**

Linux Online **www.linux.org**

Macromedia **www.macromedia.com**

MapQuest.com **www.mapquest.com**

Microsoft **www.microsoft.com**

National Association of Professional Employer Organizations **www.napeo.org**

Netscape **www.netscape.com**

Pay Plus Benefits **www.payplusbenefits.com**

PayMaxx **www.paymaxx.com**

Pinnacle Decision Systems **www.pinndec.com**

WebEx **www.webex.com**

Chapter 4

Procurement & Inventory Management

Northern Mountain Supply, a retailer of camping and outdoor equipment, is located in a beautiful part of California—close to both the Pacific Ocean and national parks and forests. But its location has a downside: The company doesn't have access to a large number of resources. Its single retail store, which has about 26 employees, opened in 1974, in Humboldt County, behind the "redwood curtain." Since it started purchasing and selling on the Internet in 1996, however, Northern Mountain has established contacts with a wide range of companies. The company buys all of its business software and other supplies through Web-based catalogs. And it has found new customers through its Web site. Result: Since 1996, sales have more than doubled.

If you are responsible for purchasing for your small or midsize company, you, too, can find supplies easily, quickly, and at low prices on the Internet. You can place orders electronically within a matter of minutes, just as larger corporations have done for years using specialized electronic data interchange systems. Going online to procure stock gives you these additional advantages:

• *Your employees can purchase their own supplies online* (with the appropriate approval).

• *You can conduct paperless procurement,* thus saving the cost and time involved in generating the usual purchasing documents.

• *You can snatch bargains by bidding on supplies at an auction.*

• *Your preferred suppliers can set up automatic inventory control systems* to help you replenish stock and set up packages of supplies based on previous orders.

Small businesses—those with from 1 to 100 employees—are flocking to the Internet to purchase goods and services. A study by Access Markets

TIP If you plan to start purchasing supplies online, begin by taking stock. Determine how much it costs your company to generate a typical supply order and how long it takes to receive what you have requested. Ask your coworkers: Are you satisfied with the current supply chain? (Such communications are ideal for an e-mail system or can be posted in the form of a Web-page survey on your intranet.)

International Partners and *Inc.* magazine shows that in 1999, businesses spent $25 billion for goods and services on the Internet—more than 12 times the amount spent the year before.

Of course, buying supplies online isn't a solution for all companies all the time. Some Web-based supply houses don't include clear photos or detailed descriptions of the products they sell. AquaPrix, a water purification system distributor in Hayward, Calif., performs administrative services through the Internet, for example, but has been reluctant to turn to purchasing online. Part of the reason for its hesitation, one company executive reported, is that some Web sites have a more limited selection than printed catalogs put out by supply superstores. Shopping carefully for the items you really need at online B2B marketplaces, however, can bring big benefits to your organization.

B2B supplier marketplaces. Supplier marketplaces—Web sites that serve as gathering spots for businesses wanting to exchange goods and services—are among the hottest e-commerce services on the Internet. These companies are usually listed by name, geographic location, or type of business. Beyond that, the marketplace Web site organizes the companies so online visitors from around the world can easily find new trade leads. Foodbuy.com, a B2B marketplace for the foodservice industry, for example, is a partnership bringing together big manufacturers such as General Mills

Foodservice, as well as smaller concerns such as Beaverton Foods, Kozy Shack, and Maplehurst Foodservice.

If you need to make new connections, broaden your market base, or get advice on business subjects, then it would be worth your time to explore supplier marketplaces. Begin by searching one of the big indexes to Web sites, such as About.com. Go to the site's front page and enter the keywords "B2B marketplace" in the search box. A page will appear with a list of links to supplier marketplaces.

You'll have even better luck finding a marketplace in your field of business by going to a site that specializes in B2B resources, such as B2Bexplorer. Click on the link labeled "Search the Business Directory," and your browser will connect to a powerful search engine that lets you search for marketplaces by category, location, contact name, business name, or keywords.

You can visit the Web sites of online marketplaces such as Commerce One's My MarketSite, Entrade, or VerticalNet to find a supplier or group of related supply companies that provide the goods you need. If you're in the hospital-supply industry, for instance, you could explore the businesses listed in the health-care section of Commerce One's My MarketSite. If you're looking for a quote on some supplies, you could post the requests for quotes (RFQs) on an online bulletin board. You might also find announcements of upcoming trade shows or links to the Web sites of trade publications in your field.

Save purchasing time. B2B supply houses, such as Works.com, one of the best-known business supply marketplaces on the Web, make it easy to shop quickly for what you need. Registering is a matter of filling out an online form with information about your company and selecting a user name and password so you can place orders securely. Shopping involves browsing an electronic catalog and selecting items for placement in an electronic shopping cart of the sort used on many consumer-retail Web sites.

Most B2B marketplaces provide multiple payment options. Compaero, a distributor of electrical connectors based in Midlothian, Va., provides components to procurement officers for agencies within the U.S. Department of Defense as well as individual military bases. This marketplace lets you pay with your credit card, C.O.D., or by means of an account you set up with the supply house before you do your shopping.

Post RFQs online. Do you have a difficult time obtaining bids or finding vendors to bid on your products? Do you need to order supplies that you have never requested before and aren't sure what constitutes a reasonable price for such items? Consider letting the market decide the price by posting an RFQ on a special Web site where suppliers can actually bid on the items you're looking for. Your quote would go to the lowest bidder. You might save money and find some new vendors as well.

Commerce One's auction feature on My MarketSite, enables companies to publish RFQs for goods and services they're interested in purchasing. Suppliers who use My MarketSite can then read the RFQs and post bids online. Such an arrangement

> **TIP** No matter how high-tech the procurement method, small businesses need to be aware that the online purchasing process—which can be completed in just a matter of minutes—can be *too* easy. Diane M. Carco, coauthor, with Brad L. Peterson, of *The Smart Way to Buy Information Technology: How to Maximize Value and Avoid Costly Pitfalls* (AMACOM, 1998), suggests that you should be sure you have an immediate need for the products you are ordering. Even though it may seem obvious, managers often try to obtain a solution to a problem before they've fully defined it, she says.

constitutes a reverse auction—in which suppliers compete for the buyer's business. LendingTree.com, another popular reverse auction site, enables consumers looking for a mortgage to get bids from lending institutions.

Besides reverse auctions, Commerce One also provides forward auction capabilities through which suppliers can auction off part of their inventory. This can be a good way to reduce stock that your company needs to get rid of.

B2B auctions. When a piece of equipment breaks down at The Great Plate Bar & Grill, in Tracy, Calif., co-owner Shawn Perry goes online to find tech support or repair manuals. The Great Plate buys plates, silverware, and copier-toner cartridges on the auction site eBay. The restaurant purchases "most everything but food" online, says Perry.

If you have ever used eBay or other consumer-auction sites on the Web, you're probably wondering what the difference is between an online B2B and a consumer auction. And you're probably wondering about other things too, such as:

• *How long do auctions last?* Auctions on eBay often last a week or more. In contrast, B2B auctions, such as those on SupplierMarket.com, are usually over in a matter of hours; sales are facilitated by software that matches buyers and sellers.

• *How trustworthy are the participants?* On eBay, anyone can be the highest bidder, and fulfilling a sale requires a level of trust. On B2B auction sites, only businesses that have registered with the marketplace service beforehand can participate in an auction.

SupplierMarket.com goes one step further and allows buyers and sellers to purchase the credit ratings of vendors, and the site's account managers also personally verify company information. The best way to check out the reputation of an auction site is to talk to some of its customers; the auction's customer service department should be able to suggest some you could contact.

If you feel a need to exercise even more control, some B2B auction sites will let you specify a starting price or even name suppliers that you would like to have included or excluded in the bidding process.

Finding new vendors. New sources of supply are emerging around the world. The Internet gives you a way to contact suppliers in newly industrialized economies in Southeast Asia or China, for instance. If your suppliers are located only in your own geographic area, you can widen your supplier base by making use of Web-based trade publications. Check out Web-based "trading zones" as well, where suppliers worldwide request quotes, bid on goods, and post notices about what they want to exchange.

When you locate a trade publication that specializes in your area of interest, look for a bulletin board or classified-ads area. Usually you'll find a Web page on which visitors can post messages for one another. Often, this is where you'll find RFQs or trade leads. You can post your own message on the bulletin board by filling out a short form.

Sometimes the trade publications you find on the Web give you insight into how business is done in a far-off part of the world. *SemiWorld*, a small-scale publication with a very specialized audience—the semiconductor industry—is based in Seoul, Korea. Its bulletin board serves that target industry.

And here are a few of the other trade publications you can find listed on Commerce One and by surfing around the Internet:

- *Aviation International News/Online,* based in Midland Park, N.J.
- *Chemical & Engineering News Online,* based in Washington, D.C.
- *PetroMin,* published in Singapore

Vendor qualifications. If you do locate potential trading partners through either online supplier Web sites or trade publications, it's important to do some research before you actually commit to doing business with them. Here, too, the Internet functions as a time-saver. You can check the vendor's

Web site (look for an "About Us" or "About Our Company" page) to get background information on the company. If your company only does business with organizations that meet a particular International Standards Organization standard, check to see whether the company has such a rating. If the company is publicly held, search for it on Yahoo!'s Web site to get stock and other financial information.

Collecting from overseas customers can be complicated, and some research on the subject beforehand will reduce your risk of losses. Ask your bank whether the foreign banks involved in the transactions are reliable and prompt; you can also consult some freight forwarders, companies that serve as the middlemen between the boat and the bank.

Checks and balances. Web-based supply houses, such as Staples.com, Works.com, and SupplierMarket.com, make purchasing so easy that practically anyone can do it—which is why it's a good idea to set up an internal chain of purchasing approval in your company. Matt St. John, who is both payables clerk and office-supply purchasing agent for Professional Cutlery Direct, a 45-employee North Branford, Conn., retailer of high-end kitchenware, has found prices on Works.com that are 5% to 66% lower than other sources. "Besides saving on prices, we also save big in terms of time," says St. John. "Works.com prints out a purchase order for us, and they also can download an invoice straight into our accounting program. Anyone with a password can go to Works.com and request supplies. Their request is then e-mailed to me for final approval. When everything is approved, the items are automatically ordered."

It has long been the province of purchasing agents to solicit competitive bids, compare proposals, and ensure that their organizations get the best deal. When the online procurement process is regulated, however, companies can save time by letting individual staff members order the supplies

> **TIP** If you seek out overseas trade contacts through the Internet, be aware of any trade restrictions that apply to your industry. You need to be especially wary if you trade in agricultural products or foodstuffs, or if your potential business partners are in countries that are subject to trade restrictions. Arent Fox Kintner Plotkin & Kahn's Web site is a good clearinghouse of recent legal information and trade issues. Also, foreign laws might complicate trade. For instance, a so-called distance-contract directive proposed by the European Union (the organization of 15 European countries), says that European consumers don't need any reason to return goods within seven days of purchase. Other directives hamstring companies that want to transmit information they've collected on customers over international boundaries.

they need. As a manager, you need to keep the following in mind:

• *It's not an either-or situation.* Professionals can handle procurement of expensive core technologies, while individuals can request paper, pencils, and other low-budget items electronically.

• *You can, and should, build oversight into the process.* Most B2B supply houses have procedures that allow a company to specify who can place an order directly and who needs to get approval first before a purchase is finalized.

Increased productivity. By leveraging technology through online purchasing from suppliers, you can increase your productivity dramatically. The volume of Chicago-based Corrugated Supplies Corp., a manufacturer of corrugated paper and cardboard, for instance, has more than doubled in the past two years, thanks in large measure to customers' ability to place orders online (see "Just-in-Time Keeps Inventory Moving," on page 44).

Professional Cutlery Direct (PCD) has many suppliers located in France. It uses e-mail to keep in touch with them, thereby saving time and money. "This has been enormously helpful," says CEO Terri Alpert.

Professional Cutlery also corresponds by e-mail with virtually all of its manufacturers' representatives to verify prices and descriptions of products. And changes or additions to Professional Cutlery's mailing list are sent to the company that processes the list using the Internet's file transfer protocol, allowing large volumes of data to be transferred quickly.

PCD's transaction processing is seamlessly integrated with purchasing, receiving, customer service, and shipping operations. This helps the company offer a huge assortment of products while still turning its inventory over 10 times a year. "We have a very low back-order rate and are able to almost always ship catalog orders whole," says Alpert.

In 1999, the company invested about $360,000, or 4% of its revenues, in technology, and Alpert planned to continue that pace to permit more Web interaction with customers. "We never could have existed as a company without e-mail and our intranet," she says. "Bigger catalog companies are always amazed at what Professional Cutlery Direct does, and how many SKUs we manage, how we keep them all in stock with very few back orders, and how many new catalogs we come out with a year. Companies with 10 times our sales cannot do as much!"

Group buying power. Companies can reduce costs substantially by joining together and using their collective purchasing power online. The independent printing companies that are part of printeralliance.com, an online B2B community, save 3% to 10% on the cost of essential supplies such as paper, ink, and chemicals. Printeralliance.com obtains substantial rebates from a limited number of respected suppliers that it chooses in each product category. Member companies benefit from the cost savings while suppliers increase their sales.

JUST-IN-TIME KEEPS INVENTORY MOVING

Corrugated Supplies Corp. (CSC), a Chicago company founded in 1964, leverages Internet technology to enable just-in-time inventory and virtual warehousing. CSC receives 700 to 800 orders for corrugated sheets daily. While many of the orders are received by phone, more than half of all customer communications take place electronically. Customers can adjust their orders electronically and even prioritize and schedule multiple orders by filling out Web-page forms on CSC's extranet, which is protected by encryption and password authentication.

The speed with which orders are entered into CSC's intranet means that its corrugator can be up and running within hours; the shipping department—which has wireless PCs with intranet access attached to its forklifts, providing customer names, addresses, and job numbers—can put orders on the trucks and have them ready to be delivered in less than 24 hours.

Managing inventory. As much as 30% of a company's assets are commonly held in inventory. Too much inventory keeps profits down; insufficient inventory hurts customer relations. Demand can vary depending on the season, the state of the economy, and many other factors. The Internet can enable you to replace stock quickly, and some Internet-based suppliers will even manage your inventory, replenishing supplies automatically.

If you can place an order on the Web in a few minutes and receive shipment on it the next day, you can reduce your inventory. With a just-in-time model, inventory is ordered only when needed. If one supplier doesn't have what you want, you simply go online to a backup.

Once you set up a direct channel with a supplier, it becomes easier to obtain

Because each order is "made to order," CSC maintains no real inventory. When customers' crews arrive in the morning, a trailer loaded with their corrugated sheets is waiting at the dock door.

Company representatives note that the customer service component of their business now includes training customers on the new Web technology and then marketing its advantages directly to them. One such advantage is that customers can find out when to expect their orders to arrive by accessing shipping information on the extranet.

The Chicago facility is now producing 200 million square feet of corrugated board each month. The efficiency with which CSC places, tracks, and fulfills its orders through the use of a Web-based intranet caused one customer to shut down its own corrugating facilities and to make CSC its sole supplier. CSC's Web-based procurement systems and state-of-the-art manufacturing facility allow it to feed the customer's five manufacturing facilities with less than 24-hour turnaround.

customized product information, technical specifications, and pricing information. Having a close online relationship with a supplier can be especially helpful if you need something in a rush or if a problem occurs with an order.

Superior Tool Co., of Brooklyn Heights, Ohio, a firm that was founded in 1947, manufactures hand tools for the plumbing industry. It uses its intranet and the Internet to distribute to all employees daily data on production, inventory levels by category, inventory adjustments, and other critical information. Such close tracking of available supply and customer orders enables the company's 20 employees to stay on top of daily trends and respond to customer inquiries in a manner—and speed—that was unimaginable just a few years ago. ■

COMPANIES AND SITES IN THIS CHAPTER

About.com **www.about.com**

Access Markets International Partners **www.ami-usa.com**

AquaPrix **www.aquaprix.com**

Arent Fox Kintner Plotkin & Kahn **www.arentfox.com**

Aviation International News **www.ainonline.com**

B2Bexplorer **www.b2bexplorer.com**

Chemical & Engineering News **www.pubs.acs.org/cen**

Commerce One's My MarketSite **www.marketsite.net**

Compaero **www.compaero.com**

Corrugated Supplies **www.vancraft.com**

eBay **www.ebay.com**

Entrade **www.entrade.com**

Foodbuy.com: **www.foodbuy.com**

General Mills Foodservice **www.generalmills.com/foodservice**

Kozy Shack **www.kozyshack.com**

LendingTree **www.lendingtree.com**

Northern Mountain Supply **www.northernmountain.com**

PetroMin **www.petromin.safan.com**

printeralliance.com **www.printeralliance.com**

SemiWorld **www.semiworld.com**

Staples **www.staples.com**

Superior Tool **www.superiortool.com**

SupplierMarket.com **www.suppliermarket.com**

The Great Plate Bar & Grill **www.thegreatplate.com**

VerticalNet **www.verticalnet.com**

Works.com **www.works.com**

Yahoo! **www.yahoo.com**

Chapter 5

Partner Networks

Sometimes the best business model does not involve marketing to millions. It involves giving special attention to specific customers. That's proven to be the case for Baltimore-based RewardsPlus, an employee benefits outsourcer that provides communication, administration, benefits, and billing to client companies. The 140-employee company provides human resources information and services to the employees of client companies who connect to a special part of the RewardsPlus Web site called an *extranet*. A client's employee logs into the RewardsPlus extranet and obtains information specific to his or her company's plan.

This Internet technology didn't come cheap: RewardsPlus originally invested $700,000 of its $2.1 million in seed capital in its Web-based benefits administration system. But the investment is helping RewardsPlus grow: The company's revenues for the first quarter of 2000 were 300% higher than those for the first quarter of 1999.

The ABCs of extranets. In an apartment building with a doorman, only residents of that building can walk through the front entrance without being stopped. They, in turn, admit the visitors they choose. An extranet works the same way: It can be viewed as part of a company's intranet that is extended to users outside the company, whether they be mobile employees, customers, or supplier companies. An extranet is a set of private Web pages that only a special group of individuals can access. For RewardsPlus, this means participants' data is kept safe behind a firewall, but authorized partners can access the information they need on the RewardsPlus extranet through their connection to the Internet.

Extranets have also been described as a state of mind: The Internet gives your company a way to do business with other companies and to sell products to customers in a way that is selective, secure, and personalized. You can use an extranet to make your B2B partners feel like an audience of one for the information you provide especially for them and no one else.

For some companies, setting up extranets is a complicated process that can involve hiring IT consultants, arranging telecommunications connections, and establishing security schemes. If you set up sophisticated secured areas, for example, ones in which participants can generate customized Web-page content on the fly, the system can easily cost tens of thousands of dollars. In 1997, a story on CNET reported that the e-commerce software developer SpaceWorks® announced it would create trial e-commerce or extranet sites for customers within 30 days for a cost of $25,000 to $50,000. Today, SpaceWorks says on its Web site that it can set up complete e-commerce solutions in 60 days, but doesn't quote such prices, which are surely low for many companies in today's market.

Keeping it simple. Fortunately, small and midsize companies that want to provide extranet access to perhaps 10 to 20 employees or clients, there are simpler alternatives that work well. An extranet can be as simple as a Web page you create for a supplier that contains a list of your current inventory. Like an unlisted phone number, you give out the URL for the page selectively. In this case, you'd give it to the supplier or customer by e-mailing it to someone at the company. No one else will know that the page exists.

When you think extranet, think targeted information. By creating an extranet, you give yourself the ability to publish content aimed at specific business partners and even individuals. By giving preferred suppliers or colleagues access via the Internet to their own area of your internal network (thus making it an extranet), you build goodwill and cement ongoing relationships. The trick is to find data that you can target to one specific set of important customers. Or, if you already expend considerable effort preparing reports or proposals for important clients, think about putting them online in a secured area of your site. Here are a few examples of what you could publish on an extranet:

- *Proposals or requests for quotes*
- *Training information that applies to specific employees*
- *Personalized customer and vendor information*

The key is to approach your information in a new way: Rather than broadcasting it to everyone over the Internet, *narrowcast* selected data to important groups in order to retain existing customers and business partners and improve collaboration.

Security considerations. It's natural to be cautious when putting financial or personnel information online. Such data needs to be protected, and simply putting out a private URL wouldn't be enough. For confidential information you need to rely on the sort of Internet-based security schemes—authentication and encryption—that are already making e-commerce and information exchange viable in cyberspace.

- *Authentication.* This is the process of requiring someone to verify that he or she is an approved user by providing a user name and password. In technical terms, this means that the directory on the Web server that holds the sensitive Web page, graphics, or other files is set up so that, whenever a visitor connects to that directory, a standard password-protection box pops up. The visitor then has to enter a user name/password pair that matches one of a set that your Webmaster has designated in order to gain entry.

To set up password protection for a part of your Web server, you'll need access to the server itself. If you run your own Web server, you'll have no problem. If you *co-locate*—that is, if you own your own Web server, but it exists on an Internet service provider's (ISP's) facility—you'll be able to go to the ISP and

TIP If you plan to provide a lot of extranet services, it makes sense to either operate your own server or make arrangements with your Web-hosting service to have script-level access to its server. Either arrangement will allow you to run your own common gateway interface (CGI) scripts, such as those that process data submitted by Web-page forms on your site.

add the protection yourself. If you outsource your server, and your Web site is a directory on a server that's actually owned and operated by an ISP or Web host, however, you'll have to ask the host if scripts can be run on your server. A program that enables scripts written in Perl or another programming language needs to be available. If one is, and you can proceed, the host must grant access to the server to someone on your staff so that he or she can place scripts in the appropriate locations.

• *Encryption.* This is the process of encoding sensitive data using a mathematical formula called an algorithm. Once encoded, information is unreadable for anyone except the intended recipient, who decodes it using a formula called a key. On the Internet, information can be encrypted at different stages in the process of transmitting it from a server to a client. Secure-sockets-layer (SSL) security is the scheme most widely used. It uses a combination of encryption and authentication schemes (see Chapter 7) and is widely considered reliable protection.

Extranet management. You can manage your extranet in-house, or you can outsource its management to a relatively new type of company called an extranet service provider. Exa Corp., a computer-aided engineering software and services company with 43 employees based in Lexington, Mass., outsourced its extranet to a branch of its telecommunications provider. Exa gives its customers the ability to conduct complex simulations of extranets that have intensive bandwidth and security requirements.

Extranets vs. virtual private networks. If you operate in an industry that relies on sensitive client information, you might consider setting up a virtual private network (VPN) instead of an extranet. Both VPNs and extranets consist of areas of an internal network that are open only to selected groups or individuals. The difference between them has to do with the degree of access that outsiders have to your data.

The two terms are often used interchangeably. In general, though, a VPN is distinguished from an extranet by its use of more complex Internet security schemes. A VPN is created in order to connect two local area networks (LANs), each of which has a gateway with security features through which outsiders can "tunnel" their way into the internal network.

A VPN often provides more secure connections than an extranet through the use of leased lines or other options. For instance, Green Mountain Energy^{SM}, an Austin, Tex.-based energy supplier, uses direct connections through frame relay to connect with suppliers and contractors. A VPN is a way to ensure privacy while using the public Internet for network infrastructure rather than a leased line.

What can you do with an extranet? Green Mountain Energy gives indi-

TIP IT personnel commonly toss around terms with *net* in them, such as *intranet*, *extranet*, and *virtual private network*, in a confusing way. As a manager, you may find it helpful to focus not on the jargon and the technical aspects of these types of networks but on the level of access you want users to have. Access is the most important distinguishing characteristic between each of these *net* terms.

Partner Networks

viduals access to a variety of specialized information through its Web site. Customers connecting to the public part of the Web site, click on the "My Account" link, and log onto the company's private, customers-only extranet. The Green Mountain network is essentially an extranet linking the company's LAN with a vast array of energy suppliers, brokers, and technology vendors. Customers can access their account information and energy-usage history. They can also choose to be billed electronically rather than by mail, thus saving the company administrative, paper, and postage costs.

The table below lists some of the content you could put on an extranet.

TYPES OF EXTRANET CONTENT

Content	Description	Degree of Technical Difficulty
Web page	A special Web page set up for individual users that has a secret URL	Simple
Downloadable files	Software programs or other files that selected users can download using their Web browsers	Simple
Content created for clients	Visitors to the extranet identify themselves by answering a series of questions; custom content is gathered from a database in response to their preferences.	Complex

New options for targeting business information. Once you expend the time, personnel, and money to set aside a secured area of your internal network for your business partners and employees, there are a number of substantial benefits. They include:
- *Real-time response*
- *Instant feedback from business partners*
- *Closer ties with business partners*

By also providing the technological infrastructure for remote access, you can give your employees and partners different ways to use your internal data, including the following:

• *E-mail access.* Sean Lewis, marketing manager with Absher Construction Co., a general contractor and construction management service firm in Puyallup, Wash., that employs more than 100 people, says that e-mail, both internally and externally, has made a "huge impact" on the speed of the company's communications. The increased efficiency, in turn, results in cost and time savings. The company also creates project-management Web sites for many of its jobs and even provides cameras on job sites so that customers can view the progress of the work over the Internet through their Web browsers.

• *Dial-up remote access.* One of the great benefits of creating an extranet or a virtual private network is that mobile workers can connect to your company's network by dialing into the Internet from a remote location. Journyx, of Austin, Tex., a Web-based, e-workforce management solutions firm with 50 employees, estimates that a full 25% of its workers telecommute.

• *Downloadable files.* Presentations done in PowerPoint by Microsoft or drawings created in Adobe Photoshop® can clog e-mail gateways when they are as large as 1MB or 2MB in size. If prospective clients or business partners who depend on 56Kbps or slower dial-up modem connections receive a

> **TIP** Don't go it alone when setting up an extranet. The directors of Green Mountain Energy℠ had to learn a new technological system when they decided to revamp their energy company and put it online in 1997. The company sought help from IT consultants—specifically, Diamond Technology Partners, a Chicago-based e-business and digital strategies firm.

file that takes 5 to 10 minutes or longer to download, that file can block their incoming e-mail. With an extranet, you can post large files on a special Web page, create a link to that page, and have your clients download the file. (Typically, to download the file a visitor would right-click on it and choose "Save File As.") Partners and clients can then save the file to disk by using their browser.

Once you open your network to selected outsiders, you can collaborate instantly on projects without having to travel physically to the same locations.

An audience of one for proposals and quotes. A set of password-protected Web pages are a convenient means of presenting proposals and requesting quotes from other vendors. Rather than printing out those reports, which are hundreds of pages in length, create a protected area and post the documents online. Clients and suppliers can easily cite the URL of a particular page if they need to refer to specific content, rather than using other time-consuming methods of citation.

Personalizing your training initiatives. Web-based training courses can save your company time and travel costs, but they lack the personal touch. By setting up an extranet that employs personalization software, you can tailor training material to your employees' level of experience and their educational and cultural backgrounds. Your human resources staff can also set up pages that are tailored to your staff members' individual needs.

Putting visitors in control. You can set up your network so that clients and business partners can actually create their own content. One of the more advanced technical functions of an extranet involves the creation of content customized to users' needs. Users fill out and submit a form citing their preferences and other information, and a script on the Web server retrieves documents from the company database that correspond to the information that the user has defined.

> **TIP** A software application called GuestTrack, by GuestTrack, Inc., lets a Web site serve up customized pages on the fly, based on database-driven customer profiles. GuestTrack works with both business-to-consumer catalog sales and business-to-business applications, such as training or intranet publishing. Unfortunately, such applications can be pricey, ranging from $3,000 to hundreds of thousands of dollars.

When you give customers and partners the power to locate and obtain their own updates and documentation on your company's network, you save time and money as well as improve your bottom line. GNP Computers' sales increased once customers could access and assemble the set of products they wanted to buy on a do-it-yourself basis on GNP's extranet. And, the number of customer service calls received by the computer and telecommunications solutions company, based in Monrovia, Calif., decreased. GNP offers sophisticated product-integration services on a national basis. The company's 140 employees, as well as its business partners, can gain remote access to the network through a VPN integrated with GNP's intranet, e-mail, and internal enterprise resource planning (ERP) systems. (ERP refers to the use of software to manage internal practices, such as finance and accounting, human resources, product ordering, and inventory management.

In addition, GNP's extranet recently attracted more interest by reselling computer- and telecommunications-related products. GNP's Extranet Library documentation gives customers easy access to online documents, including GNP computer manuals, training manuals, and software-upgrade procedures. Also, visitors can download software revisions and upgrades without waiting for a paper or CD version to be shipped to them.

Visitors gain access to the documentation in the Extranet Library by connecting to the GNP Web site through a special link that requests a user name and a password. This password-controlled link keeps the customer-specific data secure and easily accessible. This kind of personalization makes visitors feel in control and increases their level of satisfaction. ∎

COMPANIES AND SITES IN THIS CHAPTER

Absher Construction **www.abshernw.com**

Adobe Systems **www.adobe.com**

Aventail **www.aventail.com**

CNET Networks **www.cnet.com**

Diamond Technology Partners **www.diamtech.com**

Exa Corp. **www.exa.com**

GNP Computers **www.gnp.com**

Green Mountain Energy℠ **www.greenmountain.com**

GuestTrack **www.guesttrack.com**

Journyx **www.journyx.com**

Microsoft **www.miscrosoft.com**

RewardsPlus **www.rewardsplus.com**

SpaceWorks® **www.spaceworks.com**

Chapter 6

Secure Private Connections

Suppose that by opening your internal network selectively to prospective and current clients, you could take on new business and hire few or no new employees. Sound too good to be true?

Pay Plus Benefits, the professional employer organization with 10 full-time employees, has doubled its revenues over the past two years with the addition of only a handful of new people. Among other things, the Kennewick, Wash., company uses its Web site to find out how many personnel a prospective customer has on its staff, what insurance packages and 401(k) plans the company provides to its employees, and other sensitive benefits-related data. Pay Plus uses the information to draft and send quotes for services quickly, while ensuring that the customer's information remains secure.

Maximizing Security. The biggest risk associated with opening your network to outside access is that unauthorized individuals could slip in and steal sensitive data. When security is of utmost importance, consider setting up a virtual private network (VPN) for your business colleagues.

Whereas extranets allow granular access among individuals, a VPN uses the Internet to establish a connection between two local area networks (LANs). VPNs establish a secure connection by using special routers equipped with VPN software and placed at the periphery of both networks. (A router is a device that directs traffic on a network, ensuring that data gets from one point, or node, on the network to another.) The VPN software/hardware combination encrypts outgoing data and decrypts incoming traffic. It also can be configured to limit access to approved users only. (See the sections called "Protocols and Tunnels" and "VPN Software," on page 62.)

Once you set up a secure VPN connection between your company and that of a business colleague or client, you can provide them with valuable information such as job estimates, payment schedules, and job schedules during a project. The auto industry, for example, has created a buying network that connects partners and suppliers. You can also provide products such as software solutions—applications that other companies can add to their own sites or use to improve their operations.

If your company has multiple projects going on simultaneously in several remote locations, and your staff needs to keep in touch with your company's internal network, they can use their portable computers to connect to it through a VPN. At Pepper Construction of Barrington, Ill., for instance, VPN connections enable project managers on all Pepper's construction sites to communicate with the home office and with other employees.

Post proprietary material. If you are you too busy with day-to-day business activities to prepare proposals or presentations, one solution might be to prepare your presentations in Web format and post them online. You don't have to make the presentations visible to the public. Simply give your clients a secret URL or set up password authentication for the directory on the Web server that holds the presentation. Then issue a password to the company that needs to review the material.

eLabor.com, a labor and resources planning solutions firm with 200 employees and $20 million annual revenues, based in Camarillo, Calif., puts a variety of documentation online in its effort to gain new business. That documentation includes quick facts about eLabor Time, a time-tracking and billing program for chief financial officers, payroll officers, and supervisors; and an online demo of eLabor Project, a planning tool for project managers. Putting such documentation on the Web makes it possible for eLabor.com to demonstrate its products and services without having to physically visit a prospect. Not only does this reduce the time the company has to spend selling its services, but it also enables the company to focus its time and energy on the most qualified prospects for its human resources services.

Present yourself to new clients. FACTS Management, a tuition management company that has 2,000 clients in all 50 states, helps students and their families manage college, private, and parochial school tuition payments. Its goal is to help schools retain students who might drop out—and attract students who may never have enrolled—because of financial reasons. Preferred client schools and FACTS Management's 60 full-time and 40 part-time employees gain access to FACTS data through a VPN.

Through its network, FACTS's home office in Lincoln, Nebr., is able to provide updated information to its regional sales staff. Formal sales presentations are prepared and transmitted through the Internet to prospective client schools. A standardized presentation consisting of Web-page charts that demonstrate cash-flow benefits plus detailed hyperlinked Web pages have been placed on a password-protected part of the FACTS Management Web site. With a quick e-mail to a potential client with a Web link and a password, the company can deliver a good presentation quickly and easily.

Existing FACTS clients are given access to special password-protected customer-service sites that promote new services. (For a case history on FACTS, see "Firm 'Schools' Its Clients Via a VPN," on page 60.)

> **TIP** If a good percentage of your business is done overseas, consider putting some of your resources in more than one language. The Web site of Anderson & Associates, a professional engineering and design services firm based in Blacksburg, Va., includes Spanish and German text and serves as a model of how to entice foreign-language speakers to visit your site.

Provide specialized software. A growing number of businesses are using VPNs to deliver software applications to the companies with whom they do business. Although many of these companies are not usually outsourcers, by providing software they are functioning as application service providers (ASPs) and are employing a new strategy for reaching customers. ASPs host the software, and the companies they work with access that software and use it over the Internet. Clients can connect to the provider company over a VPN to perform essential business tasks such as billing, payroll, and printing without having to install software or do expensive programming.

Becoming an ASP is a complex and costly undertaking. You may need to

FIRM "SCHOOLS" ITS CLIENTS VIA A VPN

The security of its customers' and its own data is of the utmost concern to FACTS Management, a tuition management company based in Lincoln, Nebr.

In addition to FACTS's corporate firewall and password protection, client schools receive special software that establishes a fully encrypted and protected link over the company's VPN. Schools are able to connect to an area of the FACTS Management Web site called InstaFACTS, where they can retrieve reports on the students whose tuition payment plans are being administered by FACTS Management. Such reports include account histories, as well as information about projected and missed payments.

School administrators can connect to InstaFACTS to change or update their own organization's information on the network, such as payment amount or parent plan. Students enrolled at schools that use FACTS Management's services can enter a user name and password and apply for a special SCHOLAR Loan on the company's Web site.

hire programmers who can develop Web-based services or applications. If you already have applications that your company has created and uses for your own accounting, inventory, or human resources functions, consider making them available to your B2B partners on an ASP basis.

In many cases, B2B companies have created applications that their business partners can use online. GNP Computers, a computer telecommunications solutions provider in Monrovia, Calif., makes a program called the Custom Product Configurator that enables visitors to its Web site to fill out a form specifying exactly what type of features they want in a server. Product inquiries and sales have increased as a result. The Web site and intranet of

> "Our client schools benefit because they can look at information about what we are doing at any time, night or day," says Randall Bretz, vice-president for customer service. "It also gives them up-to-the-minute information rather than weeks-old paper reports. At one level or another, our clients can change virtually any piece of information we have in their area. Access is also available via phone, mail, and fax. However, the online access is far quicker and easier."
>
> Giving clients control over some of the company's internal information empowers those clients, but control is not granted without adequate training and customer service. "Training for your customers is vital," Bretz emphasizes. "You can't just give them the program and expect that they will take the time to load and learn. Initially we just gave them the disks. Next we found we were sending sales staff to install and train. We now guide clients through implementation and provide training via phone, online, and interactive CD."

The Advanced Group of Cos., a full-service staffing firm in Deerfield, Ill., handle order intake and fulfillment, tracking, and invoicing.

Protocols and tunnels. A VPN uses one of several special *protocols*, as well as encryption, to give added protection to data. A protocol is a set of standard instructions that enable computers to communicate with one another over a network regardless of the operating system and hardware characteristics of the individual units.

To set up a VPN you will need software that supports a tunneling protocol. One of the most widely used protocols (popular because it is supported by Microsoft in Windows NT/4.0 and Windows 98) is point-to-point tunneling protocol. A tunnel is the entry point at each end of the connection. The connection can be made to either an individual computer or a LAN. Typically, the connection passes through a firewall, and information is encrypted to ensure security and privacy.

Another protocol is IPSec. This protocol is specifically designed to provide security for VPNs through a particularly strong set of Internet security schemes, including the exchange of long encryption codes called public and private keys; algorithms such as MD5, for authenticating packets of data; and the exchange of digital certificates.

If you want to set up a VPN, you'll need to purchase hardware and/or software such as TunnelMaster, developed by Network TeleSystems, that creates a tunnel between your private network and the public Internet through the use of one of these protocols.

VPN software. You'll also need to obtain and install special VPN software. In most cases, this software is integrated with hardware devices. It is sometimes built into routers, for instance. Or it can be located elsewhere on the network, so that if a router on the gateway fails (there is typically more than one router), the VPN does not also fail as a result. VPN software comprises a number of Internet-based security components, including:

- *A security-policy server.* This server maintains the access-control lists and other user-related information. One example is a RADIUS server.
- *A certificate server.* This server verifies the digital certificates that users are issued.

A digital certificate is a code issued to an individual or group by a certificate authority (CA) to ensure the identity of the certificate holder. Some large companies set up their own certificate servers and act as their own CAs. For smaller businesses, it makes sense to outsource the certificate tasks to a third-party CA. VeriSign, a leading CA, has a product called "Go Secure! for VPNs" that automates the certificate-distribution process for businesses.

You also might consider all-in-one VPN software solutions such as PowerVPN by Axent Technologies. PowerVPN, which retailed for about $2,000 at the time of this book's publication, can be installed as a stand-alone server for a VPN. There's also RaptorMobile client software, which gets installed on each computer that accesses the system.

How do you integrate networks? In order to use a VPN to communicate securely with business suppliers and partners, you need to connect your internal network—which is open to approved users only—to the external Internet, which is open to the public.

The connection point between these two types of networks is called a *gateway* and is set up using a combination of hardware and software. The

> **TIP** For small and midsize companies, it can be cost effective to purchase a single product that integrates a firewall and a VPN. Look for products that include dual power supplies and fail-over features to ensure reliability. Such safeguards make devices more expensive, but the reliability is worth it.

Private Security

63

hardware might include a router. The software can include an authentication program, a proxy server program, or special VPN software that encrypts data and possibly does authentication as well.

Once you have created a virtual network and set up security, you would typically create a *portal*, a Web page that functions as an entry point for all users, whether that includes the public, your own group of employees and business partners, or both.

Should you do it yourself? You should consider building an extranet yourself only if you already have the staff available to handle the many different tasks involved. If you do construct a VPN yourself—which entails setting up your own gateway hardware—you can expect to pay from $5,000 to $10,000 for the dedicated gateway hardware and software.

If you already have the hardware and software that creates a firewall, you can save some money by installing VPN software on an existing Web server. Such software typically costs $2,000 to $5,000. In order to install the software, you have to own and operate the Web server yourself, rather than leasing the Web server space from an Internet service provider.

Outsourcing a VPN. Smaller companies that are short on time, money, or technology should consider outsourcing a VPN. Instead of going through the considerable effort of buying, installing, and maintaining VPN products, let someone else do it for you. Imperito Networks's InstantVPN software, for example, enables you to set up a VPN in a single afternoon. At $200 per month per VPN and $10 per user (the first five are free), Imperito is a relatively affordable alternative. Imperito centrally hosts your VPN, handling the management, servers, authentication, and so on. As the administrator, you control user access through a Web browser.

RewardsPlus, an online provider of outsourced employee benefits, leases its VPN from its telecommunications provider for about $800 a month.

The VPN is central to the benefits company's entire operation. RewardsPlus offers an à la carte selection of nontraditional benefits to client companies looking to attract or retain employees. The portfolio of products (from 30 different underwriters) sold under the RealLife Benefits brand includes benefits such as automobile and homeowners insurance, mortgages, home equity loans, legal services, and pet insurance. Employees of client companies access the aggregated insurance information over a VPN.

Access for mobile/wireless users. Extranets and VPNs are not just for customers. A company's remote and mobile employees can use them, too. By setting up an extranet or other remote access connection using the Internet, you use the Net to do the work over the public infrastructure. Some businesses use a VPN to eliminate the need for a remote-access server, thus enabling mobile users to communicate with the home LAN through the Internet. ■

COMPANIES AND SITES IN THIS CHAPTER

The Advanced Group of Cos. **www.advancedgroup.com**

Anderson & Associates **www.andassoc.com**

Axent Technologies **www.axent.com**

eLabor.com **www.elabor.com**

FACTS Management **www.factsmgt.com**

GNP Computers **www.gnp.com**

Imperito Networks **www.imperito.com**

Microsoft **www.microsoft.com**

Network TeleSystems **www.nts.com**

Pay Plus Benefits **www.payplusbenefits.com**

RewardsPlus **www.rewardsplus.com**

VeriSign **www.verisign.com**

Private Security

Chapter 7

Internet Security

Data theft and security violations are real; fear of their occurrence is by no means a paranoid concern. As the Internet grows in popularity, security risks become more and more acute. Information is the coin of the Internet realm and the Net's most valuable business commodity. Your job is to set up systems that use Internet security technology to protect that commodity from hackers, thieves, and other unauthorized intruders.

If you are in the financial, insurance, or research industries, or if you do work with the government, Internet security is even more critical. At The Motley Fool, the financial services firm, security of customer data is essential: If customers feel secure, they will post more of their financial portfolios on the company's Web site. Security is important to its employees as well. A number of staff people work remotely and need to communicate on a regular basis with staff at the home office, often about the financial topics that are explored on the company's Web site. Inventory, sales, and billing information kept on the company's back-end servers need to be protected as well. The Motley Fool employs a variety of Internet security tools to protect its data, including secure sockets layer (SSL) encryption, which makes data unreadable to anyone but an authorized recipient. The company's site contains an extensive privacy statement that explains in detail the kind of personal information it gathers and how that information is used.

What can go wrong? In an Internet-based, client/server environment, in which a lot of information can be accessed by employees and possibly by people outside the company, the opportunities for disaster are manifold. The first step is to understand what can go wrong, so you can devise systems for preventing such problems.

- *Theft of customer information.* After customer credit-card numbers and other data became public for only a brief period of time on the Global Health Trax's site, five of the company's 3,500 distributors reportedly cancelled their contracts. CD Universe suffered a security breach involving a hacker who posted 25,000 credit-card numbers. It resulted in thousands of individuals flooding their respective credit-card companies with cancellation notices. Both security breaches could have been worse.

• *Theft of company resources.* Potomac Interactive Corp., a Web-site development and Internet consulting company based in Arlington, Va., discovered that hackers had used one of its servers as a repository for 500MB of stolen Macintosh software. The hackers posted the server's address on an online bulletin board, allowing others to access the software. The intrusion could have been more serious if Potomac had not installed a security system called a *firewall* to protect its internal network from unauthorized intrusion from the Internet. (The security breach occurred on a server not protected by the firewall.)

• *Virus attacks.* The "Melissa," "I Love You," and other viruses distributed by e-mail are hard to stop. Once they are discovered and their method of proliferation is publicized, however, a firewall can be configured to stop them from entering a company's internal network, where they can destroy files, tie up e-mail systems, and damage operating systems.

A comprehensive security system for a business starts with password-authentication protection for a directory and includes more sophisticated measures, such as certificates and encryption. It's important to assess your needs and undertake the implementation of security measures in a step-by-step way that keeps employees in the loop.

Develop a security policy. The first, and in many ways the most effective, way of ensuring the security of your Internet-based network is to assemble the key players on your staff to create a strategy. Introduce the problem. You want to open your network to other businesses in order to conduct B2B transactions, but customers won't make use of a network unless they feel it's secure enough to protect their personal information. Discuss possible solutions, such as:

- *Keeping sensitive information off the network altogether*
- *Wiping clean any computers that store customer data each night, or on a periodic basis*
- *Setting up a firewall*
- *Setting up authentication*
- *Using SSL security, including encryption and certificates*

Whichever route you choose, the result should be a coherent security policy that includes employee policies on password selection and use, procedures for keeping data confidential, and monitoring network use. Any security initiative that does not include these elements risks failure.

User authentication. One of the most effective ways to protect part of a Web site—either an internal intranet or an e-commerce or other external site—is through *authentication*. Authentication—the process of identifying persons through a user name and password—is widespread and relatively easy to implement (compared with SSL encryption or certificates). It's a must for small and midsize business sites. Requiring business colleagues and remote employees to log in not only protects your data, but also provides you with a record of who accesses your site and how often they visit.

Smart cards. Smart cards resemble ATM cards in that they let authorized users log onto a system through a network from the road or from home. (Such technology is also available in a disk-based format called *virtual smart cards*.) Smart cards are more secure than authentication, but they're not free of problems. For one thing, they require swipe readers. For another, setting up a swipe-card system for a business is an expensive proposition.

And smart cards are not ideal for extranet applications, because you have to issue cards to colleagues outside the company who must also install swipe readers and the accompanying software.

Biometrics. In the future, authenticating individuals may well involve the processing of their biological data: recognition of a user's speech patterns (the user would speak into a microphone in the computer), the image of a user's face captured by a digital camera and transmitted to your company, or perhaps even some form of fingerprint identification.

A major benefit of biometrics identification systems is that they can be used when PCs are unavailable. Although not widespread, such systems are already available. Quintet, of Cupertino, Calif., sells a signature-recognition package that works with handheld PCs.

Firewalls. One of the most common security strategies for companies that provide extranet access to preferred customers, remote employees, and partners is a firewall. A firewall is hardware or software that is placed on the periphery of an organization's network. All traffic going into the internal network from the Internet is screened by the firewall, which prevents unauthorized users from entering and accessing protected information.

A firewall performs essential B2B security functions, such as these:

• *Screening all incoming and outgoing traffic* by checking the IP address of each user to make sure only company employees gain access to the internal network. An IP address is a unique identifier for each computer on the network. Computers in a company that has its own Internet domain typically have blocks of IP addresses, but those addresses begin with the same series of numbers. A company that has 30 computers with access to the Internet, for instance, might have the IP addresses 128.133.47.1 through 128.133.47.30. A router or a software program that is part of a company's gateway can be configured to admit only IP addresses that begin with 128.133.47, for example.

- *Encrypting outgoing data and decrypting incoming data.*
- *Authenticating users* so only those who enter an approved password and user name gain access to the internal network.

A firewall can include an organization's VPN software. It can also exist separately from the VPN functions, providing an additional level of security for the organization it protects.

Most firewalls monitor the use of your system and keep activity logs, so you'll know if anyone is trying to break in. If someone tries to log on to your system more than three times with the wrong password, for example, the firewall's activity report will show that. (Some firewalls e-mail or page the systems administrator when they detect suspicious activity.) Other firewalls offer encryption options that allow you to scramble the information in files, making it unreadable to all but approved users.

Setting up a firewall can be a complex operation, especially if you are using hardware, such as routers, as well as software. It's worthwhile to hire a systems administrator or other technical specialist to set up the system for you. Configuring the system yourself can consume several days' worth of

> **TIP** e-Gap, developed by Whale Communications in Fort Lee, N.J., enables you to keep data—not just customer-related information, but all company information—physically separate from the Internet. e-Gap isolates your internal servers from the Internet and moves data between the internal network and the Internet by writing data to a storage device, called an e-disk. The e-disk resides between two servers, one located on your internal network, the other connected to the Internet. The data never resides on a computer that is connected to the Internet.

staff time, presuming your workers have the appropriate expertise.

For some small businesses, a software-only firewall is an affordable and relatively simple starting point. Aspen Publishers, a $60-million health and legal publishing company in Gaithersburg, Md., installed FireWall/Plus from Network-1 Security Solutions. The company wanted employees to be able to use e-mail and the Internet, but prevent outsiders from sending files into the company through the Web.

> **TIP** If you run a small or home-based business where you don't use a LAN, you still may need a firewall. "Always on" Internet connections, such as DSL or cable, are extremely vulnerable to hackers and should be protected.

Another software firewall, called eSafe Gateway, is manufactured by Aladdin Knowledge Systems. Firewalls cost from $5,000 to $15,000, depending on the number of users. Less expensive firewalls are also available to protect individual workstations or to separate one part of a network from another.

Proprietary networks. If the information you are sharing is strictly confidential, the best way to protect it is by using your own proprietary network and electronic data interchange (EDI). It's safer than an Internet-based system. Although this book promotes Internet technology, it should be noted that some companies still rely on EDI when extra security is essential. For instance, ATP Oil & Gas, an energy development and production company based in Houston, receives up-to-the-minute commodity prices through a proprietary EDI network. On the other hand, it informs its customers of quantities delivered through a proprietary network that uses secure Internet interfaces.

Encryption: the basics. Encryption is central to Web security. (The term refers to the process of transforming a series of letters or numerals that are understandable into something unrecognizable by processing the contents with a mathematical formula called an algorithm. The encoded data can be decoded only by someone who has the correct formula, called a *key*.) The potentially confusing thing is that keys, themselves, are long series of encoded numerals and letters. They vary in size depending on the degree of security being used. Some keys consist of 40 bits of data. (A data bit is an individual unit of digital information). A more powerful variety contains 128 bits of data.

In a popular form of online security called public-key encryption, you purchase a license to use a security algorithm and use that algorithm to generate a private key. With your own private key, you can then generate separate public keys. You would issue public keys to visitors who wish to access a secure area of your Web site, and the keys are issued to the visitors through their Web browsers. Their browsers encode the sensitive personal information that they send to you. You (and only you) can decode the encoded information you receive, using your original private key.

Certificates. Digital certificates are electronic documents that confirm the identity of the individual or company that owns them. In the context of B2B communications on an extranet, certificates function like private-label passports: They are issued by an authority that usually represents the data owner or owners and are given to a user or class of users, who then present them to certify their right to access a site. The best known authority of digital certificates is VeriSign.

Digital certificates are relatively cheap, transparent to the end user (once the initial qualification and software download have been completed), and easy to manage. They can be issued or revoked to whole classes of users or applications with the click of a mouse. Any organization, team, or individual can issue its own certificates, and any group can agree to share a common certificate authority, mutually authenticating one another's users.

> **TIP** If you're looking for a way to exchange encrypted e-mail messages and files with your suppliers and customers, check out products from PGP, Inc., a company formed by the author of the well-known personal encryption program Pretty Good Privacy, or PGP. One program, called PGP VPN, is designed to work with a virtual private network. Another, PGP E-Business Server, provides encryption for an entire office.

SSL. Secure sockets layer has become the *de facto* standard for Web security and is built into all major Web servers and browsers. SSL is a protocol for data transmission on the Web that combines a number of separate security methods. An SSL-protected data transaction involves the exchange of public and private keys. In addition to encryption, SSL also makes use of digital certificates.

When a user connects to a site that uses SSL, the site sends the user its certificate and an encryption formula. The site's server and the user's browser exchange a series of keys. Using these keys, the SSL-enabled site authenticates itself to the user's browser and encrypts his data.

A company engaged in B2B commerce can configure its Web site to support SSL security by buying software that integrates SSL into its intranet Web server. Look into Stronghold, developed by C2Net Software. (Stronghold works with intranets that use the free server program Apache.) Another option is iPlanet Web Server, Enterprise Edition, which supports SSL.

Encrypted tunnels. In VPNs, data passes through connection points called tunnels. A tunnel, in this context, is the particular path a message or file travels through the Internet. As it travels from the originating network and passes through the tunnel, data is encrypted. It is decrypted when it passes through the tunnel at the destination point. TunnelMaster, developed by

Network TeleSystems, is a hardware device that supports encryption and is used to create tunnels. For a version that connects to a stand-alone workstation, the cost at the time of this writing is more than $6,000.

Fit the security scheme to your data. Of all the Internet security options mentioned in this chapter, which one is right for you? Keep two principles in mind:

- *You can use multiple security methods.* You don't have to stick with a one-size-fits-all solution. You can protect some information with password authentication and other, more sensitive data with digital certificates, hardware tokens, or additional security measures.

- *More protection means less access.* The more security you employ, the longer it takes to access the information that's being protected, and the fewer the number of people who can access it.

The key to choosing the right security scheme is a data inventory. Write down a list of the data you have and rank how thoroughly it needs to be protected. Then fit the need to the appropriate security method. ■

COMPANIES AND SITES IN THIS CHAPTER

Aladdin Knowledge Systems
www.ealaddin.com

Apache Software Foundation
www.apache.com

Aspen Publishers www.aspenpub.com

ATP Oil & Gas www.atpog.com

C2Net Software www.c2net.com

CD Universe www.cduniverse.com

Corrugated Supplies www.vancraft.com

Global Health Trax www.ghtonline.com

iPlanet E-commerce Solutions
www.iplanet.com

The Motley Fool www.fool.com

Network TeleSystems www.nts.com

Network-1 Security Solutions
www.network-1.com

PGP www.pgp.com

Quintet www.quintet.com

VeriSign www.verisign.com

Whale Communications
www.whalecommunications.com

Chapter 8

Online Communities

ATP Oil & Gas Corp., a 23-employee energy development and production company based in Houston, needed to broaden its market base for sales of natural gas. But it was difficult to market to prospective customers in certain countries because of trade barriers or poor communications systems. No single marketplace existed where gas pipeline owners and customers could meet one another. ATP did some "mining" for new technology and determined that the Internet was one of the best vehicles for businesses wanting to cross geographic and cultural boundaries.

So the company turned to a tried-and-true Internet technology that even predates the Web: online bulletin boards. ATP could post messages electronically that Internet users could read and respond to. ATP's new strategy was perfect for building communities of users who shared a common interest.

The Electronic Pipeline Bulletin Boards, which were created by ATP, enable the company to access information on potential natural gas end users and to market to those customers. They also give ATP the ability to connect pipelines with hundreds of customers who, in many cases, formerly had been excluded from the company's markets. Not coincidentally, ATP ranked No. 21 on the 1999 *Inc.* 500 list of the nation's fastest growing small businesses, with a five-year growth rate of 5,073%. In 1998, the company had sales of $21,777,000, up from $421,000 in 1994.

Why join a B2B community? If you've been encountering difficulties finding buyers and vendors in your industry, consider finding new markets and making B2B connections by joining a vertical community. A vertical online trading community is a place on the Internet (usually a Web site) that presents sellers with a way to advertise their goods and services and gives buyers a way of requesting what they need. Vertical online communities are devoted to specialized areas such as energy, building materials, and clothing. Online communities might include bulletin boards that give participants a way to post messages, but it also contains Web pages that list items for sale, hyperlinks to members' Web sites, and other Internet communication features.

Many online trading communities are specially designed for B2B transactions. Such vertical communities bring together businesses in a particular field. By joining—or possibly even starting—an online community, you can:

- *Increase sales leads*
- *Find new markets*
- *Make valuable business contacts*
- *Mine valuable data about supply and demand in your field*

Finding potential clients. Amgen, a biotechnology company in Thousand Oaks, Calif., was about to release a hot new hepatitis-C drug, Infergen. The company needed to do market research on the medicine to learn about possible side effects and compliance problems that patients might have with it. So it hired Sapient Health Network (SHN), which is now a part of WebMD, to create a virtual community of hepatitis-C patients—a place where people who could potentially benefit from the drug could post messages for one another. Amgen, which projected that it would take three months to attract 500 people to the new site, was astonished to find that it took only three weeks for 500 hepatitis-C patients to join the community. Before long, membership jumped to 10,000, and Amgen was projecting that it would soon have a significant percentage of *all* hepatitis sufferers connecting to its new online resource. The project also contributed to SHN's subsequent success as a creator of online communities and provider of market data about groups of patients. Data-rich communities helped SHN to realize revenues of $6 million in 1999, a sharp rise from $1.9 million the year before.

Breaking into overseas markets. You might be surprised to learn that virtual "trade zones" have already been set up online. Few markets have as much potential as China, for example, and ChinaMallUsa.com is an online portal to that market. With bricks-and-mortar offices in New York and Beijing, ChinaMallUsa.com is an entry point on the Web that links buyers and suppliers, providing potential international trading partners with access to a comprehensive database of company profiles and product offerings from Chinese suppliers.

> **TIP** To find trade resources for various parts of the world, turn to one of the sites that attempts to organize the contents of the entire Internet, such as Yahoo! and About.com, and do a search by entering keywords such as *trade, trade in agriculture,* or *trade in Africa,* for example.

Bartering for goods and services. Online communities aren't new. In fact, discussion groups were flourishing long before the World Wide Web was even created. The first large-scale communities of computer users were hosted by the online services America Online (AOL), CompuServe, and Prodigy. What's new is how businesses, not just individuals, are using communities to trade with one another in supplies or excess inventory.

Consider the age-old activities of bartering and trading. Like streamlining administrative procedures, bartering is a way to improve your company's bottom line that doesn't involve the usual cash transactions. Get used to paying with something other than money—such as equipment or services—and saving money in the long run. BigVine.com, for example, offers individual entrepreneurs and smaller businesses the opportunity to obtain all kinds of goods and services, including office and computer equipment, through credits earned by using the services of the site. By performing a service or selling tangible products on BigVine, you earn an amount of the site's internal currency, called Trade Dollars. The exact amount of Trade Dollars you receive depends on the price you charge or what price you and the buyer agree on through negotiation. You can then use your Trade Dollars to trade for goods and services advertised on the BigVine site. Often, these are things that you wouldn't be able to afford at a regular retail outlet.

Advertising your goods or services on BigVine takes only a few minutes. The site charges a transaction fee of 3% to 4% for each sale or purchase (payment of the fee is shared between buyer and seller). The minimal charge can be worth it if you need to drum up new business. Equipment traded on BigVine can be reported as business expenses for tax purposes, but the sales you make have to be reported as taxable income. If you are listed on BigVine or similar community sites, also be prepared for an increased volume of e-mail inquires asking who you are and what you do.

Connecting with special-interest customers. Suppose you have some excess inventory, and you're willing to accept less than full retail price for it. The trick is finding the right business customers—the ones who need exactly the things you want to unload. Traditional distribution channels for surplus supplies are often time-consuming and inefficient. You might look through B2B directories and spend several valuable work hours making phone calls and faxing out product descriptions.

The same Internet that brings together buyers and sellers of virtually every imaginable product on sites such as eBay and online e-commerce stores provides gathering places for far-flung businesses that need to trade in offbeat, hard-to-find items. By joining a B2B marketplace you can list items for sale and find just the businesses that want them.

Finding the latest or most appropriate B2B marketplace for you might take a little digging. You can search on Internet index sites such as Yahoo!

or About.com, but it's more effective to look at sites that specifically collect news and information on B2B matters. Go to VerticalNet and click on the link "Business Communities." A Web page will appear with a search box in which you can enter a word or phrase related to the type of businesses you're researching, as well as a link leading to a comprehensive list of all B2B communities on VerticalNet. (At press time, the site listed more than 50 communities, each with its own marketplace.)

Posting messages on online bulletin boards. Bulletin boards are especially popular on online auction sites such as eBay, but they are a primitive means of conducting group discussions on the Internet: Each message is posted by its sender on a bulletin board Web page. The messages appear one after another in the order in which they were submitted. Messages that pertain to a single subject aren't necessarily organized by topic, and they don't always follow one another sequentially.

Bulletin board technology is especially effective, however, for communicating with companies that have e-mail or file transfer protocol (FTP) capability but aren't yet up to speed on higher-end Internet technologies like chat or videoconferencing. Not to mention it's downright enjoyable to be able to "talk" on the bulletin boards with people you get to know well. That goes for business as well as personal contacts.

The first sections of the online version of *The Wall Street Journal* to elicit a positive response from readers were its bulletin boards and discussion forums. Those resources allowed readers to talk about stories in the news. David Flores, director of the newspaper's interactive community, says that discussions commonly last as long as several months.

Being a player in discussion groups. Businesses can create discussion groups internally for their own employees, or participate in groups in Usenet—the popular designation for the part of the wider Internet that consists solely of such groups. Sometimes called *newsgroups*, discussion groups are organized by topic. Both bulletin boards and discussion groups give participants the ability to post messages that can be read—and responded to—by anyone who connects to the group. The difference is one of organization. It's much easier for participants in a discussion group to post and read a series of messages, or a *thread*, on a single subject than it is on a bulletin board.

Microsoft FrontPage 2000 gives you a way to set up internal discussion groups that are hosted on your intranet's Web server and that can be accessed only by members of your own organization. One group might be set up for discussing personnel issues, another for long-term projects, and another for social events. In order to create such groups, your network administrator has to equip your Web server with special software called FrontPage Server Extensions.

Collaborating on virtual workshops. The ability of individuals to collaborate on joint projects using e-mail, discussion groups, and bulletin boards is one of the biggest benefits of the Internet. Don't be reluctant to include freelancers, at-home workers, and remote employees in virtual project meetings. Virtual teams of coworkers can prove just as productive as staff located in the same facility.

Faced with massive traffic tie-ups in Atlanta during the 1996 Olympic Games, nearly half of the 45 employees at the accounting firm Porter Keadle Moore LLP—approximately 40 of whom commonly worked from the field, anyway—decided to work from home. Employees did not go into the office for a month; one partner commented that he hardly saw any of his coworkers during that entire period. Although it may be an extreme example, it's interesting to note that Porter Keadle Moore's employees already had laptops, and the company had e-mail and internal discussion groups that facilitated remote communication. Employees kept working rather than falling behind schedule. They did it by dialing in to their office network and collaborating on projects online until the road traffic tie-ups subsided.

When speed is key. "Real-time" communications can mean real revenues for businesses that use the Internet. Atkinson-Baker, a court reporting firm based in Glendale, Calif., knows this well. The company, which has about 95 employees, heavily promotes its ability to broadcast court reporters' notes in real time—as they are being transcribed—by using software that translates shorthand into English, then making the notes available to lawyers on the Internet.

If your business involves negotiation, bartering, or explaining your services to other businesspeople, consider real-time communications venues on the Internet such as chat rooms, videoconferencing, and virtual meeting places.

Another Internet communications strategy you can use is one-to-many rather than one-to-one. Sometimes (as is the case with chat) these communications are in the form of plain-text messages you type into your computer. In videoconferencing, though, participants can see one another on their computer screens, through technology that employs digital cameras.

Why go to the trouble of learning how to enter and use a chat room, or why type messages when you can just use the telephone? One reason is cost. With chat, you don't pay for the cost of a long-distance phone call, only the charge of connecting to your Internet service provider (ISP), if you have a dial-up connection. (If you have a direct connection there are no extra charges for making long-distance connections through your computer, only what your provider already charges you for Internet access.)

Another reason is the ability of such technological innovations to help you make new contacts. You might not be able to access some individuals by telephone. And you can always supplement your high-tech messaging with "old-fashioned" phone calls later on.

Other reasons for getting up to speed on chat technology and real-time communication include eliminating telephone tag and knowing that your message will reach the recipient just as soon as he or she checks messages or is alerted automatically by the software on his or her computer.

Chat and messaging. No, they're not just for teenagers or video game enthusiasts. Business chats are increasingly popular, especially those that enable managers to pose questions to financial and other experts.

Chat areas are set up in one of three ways:

• *By purchasing and installing chat software,* such as ichat, developed by KOZ.com, that lets you run a chat event on your own server. (This method is expensive and labor-intensive.)

• *By setting up a private chat room on a public chat service,* such as City News or Yahoo!. (This is easy and free, but gives you no control over the look and feel of the room.)

• *By outsourcing the service* to a business such as Talk City, which sets up and manages chat rooms for you. (Such a service helps you with marketing by announcing your chats on its site.)

SenseNet, an integrated software solutions provider located in Manhattan's Silicon Alley, provides chat for its clients. SenseNet itself has used chat to confer with a client about an Internet ad campaign. Employees can discuss the client's banner ads while viewing them in the chat window. Such discussions eliminate the need for more expensive videoconferencing options and save on long-distance phone charges.

Instant messaging, a variation of chat, is becoming increasingly popular for B2B conferences. One of the most popular programs is called ICQ (pronounced "I Seek You."), manufactured by ICQ Inc. Internet users whose computers are equipped with ICQ can tell when fellow ICQ users are online and can contact them instantly. If you need to provide up-to-the-minute technical support or advice to your suppliers and partners and want to give them a direct channel to you at any time, look into ICQ. IT professionals and other technical specialists demonstrate a particular fondness for ICQ, but it probably won't replace the cellular phone as the business tool of choice for upper management.

While chat and instant messaging involve text messages that you type in with your keyboard, other Internet strategies let you use your computer to communicate by video or telephone.

> **TIP** Videoconferencing is still a potentially complex and expensive technology that makes sense for small businesses only under certain circumstances. Small companies should undertake Internet-based videoconferencing only if their employees or important partners are spread out over a wide area and they need to hold meetings with them on a regular basis.

Videoconferencing. Videoconferencing enables participants to view video images of, and talk to, other individuals in real time through their computers. To make videoconferencing work, you need (at the very least) video cameras connected to the computers of each individual who will participate in the conference. You also need a broadband connection (such as DSL, T1, or frame relay) that transmits video signals fast enough so that the picture doesn't appear choppy or lag far behind the voice of the person who is speaking and whose image is being shown. You also need two additional items:

- *Videoconferencing software.* If you want to do videoconferencing through your computer, you'll need to install software that lets you send and receive video through the Internet, such as Microsoft NetMeeting or CUseeMe, by CUseeMe Networks.

- *A host.* Everyone who participates in a videoconference connects to a central hosting service on the Internet that relays the video signals. Or, a company signs up with an application service provider, such as WebEx, which hosts virtual meetings for you.

Conferencing software. Companies are discovering that there are multiple advantages to using conferencing software, such as Microsoft's NetMeeting. You can find NetMeeting bundled with the Windows 2000 operating system, or you can download it for free from Microsoft's Web site. Two or more users who have NetMeeting installed on their computers and who are connected to the Internet can communicate in several ways:

• *Chat.* They can type messages to one another and view the resulting "conversations" in the NetMeeting window.

• *Audio.* They can speak through computer microphones and hear one another's voices.

• *Whiteboard.* NetMeeting users can share drawings and diagrams that they can see at the same time.

• *Videoconferencing.* Users who have cameras attached to their respective computers can see one another on their computer screens.

• *Program sharing.* NetMeeting gives Internet users the ability to share the same computer program.

eLabor.com, the Camarillo, Calif., company that provides labor and resources planning, demonstrates its services to prospective clients using NetMeeting. "In the future, we are looking at other techniques, such as streaming video, recorded seminar sessions, and videoconferencing," comments chief technology officer Mike Toma.

Anderson & Associates, a professional engineering and design services firm with more than 160 employees, based in Blacksburg, Va., holds virtual meetings on the Internet using NetMeeting. Such conferences make sense because the company has six offices, and its clients are located in Tennessee,

North Carolina, West Virginia, and Virginia. If Anderson & Associates engineers land a job with a local government to design an improved roadway, for instance, they can refer the client to the company Web site, where the client can download NetMeeting.

Once the client and the project manager at Anderson & Associates have the same software, they can simultaneously view documents, such as specifications, drawings, pictures, diagrams, and cost estimates, over the Internet.

Internet telephony. One of the newest buzzwords in the B2B Internet technology field is voice-over Internet protocol (VoIP), which lets you place telephone calls through the Internet using computers that are equipped with sound cards, microphones, speakers, and VoIP software. (A sound card is a hardware device that plugs into a slot inside a computer and enables the machine to play audio.) However, you should explore this alternative only if you need to save money on long-distance charges and if audio communication with particular customers or partners is central to your business.

On Air Digital Audio, of Calgary, Alberta, sells audio voice-over talent to corporate clients who need broadcast-quality recordings for advertisements, narrations, and other presentations. On Air Digital Audio, which had sales of $900,000 in 1999, records both voice samples of its bank of 250 actors and custom audio clips for clients. The company, which was named one of the top 20 small-business Web sites on the Internet by *Inc. Technology* magazine, delivers clips to its clients on its Web site by downloading the files to the clients' phone systems, or via e-mail, FTP, or extranet.

The Internet has always been about bringing people together. While you may not have an immediate need to deliver audio or video to business partners and customers, knowing about the available options for getting in touch will widen your capacity to meet other businesspeople online and help your employees connect with one another in B2B collaborations. ∎

COMPANIES AND SITES IN THIS CHAPTER

About.com **www.about.com**
America Online **www.aol.com**
Amgen **www.amgen.com**
Anderson & Associates **www.andassoc.com**
Atkinson-Baker **www.depo.com**
ATP Oil & Gas **www.atpog.com**
BigVine.com **www.bigvine.com**
ChinaMallUsa.com **www.chinamallusa.com**
City News **www.citynews.com**
CompuServe Interactive Services **www.compuserve.com**
CUseeMe Networks **www.cuseeme.com**
eBay **www.ebay.com**
eLabor.com **www.elabor.com**

ICQ **www.icq.com**
KOZ.com **www.ichat.com**
Microsoft **www.microsoft.com**
On Air Digital Audio **www.onair.ca**
Porter Keadle Moore **www.pkm.com**
Prodigy Communications **www.prodigy.com**
Sapient Health Network **www.shn.net**
SenseNet **www.sensenet.com**
Talk City **www.talkcity.com**
VerticalNet **www.verticalnet.com**
The Wall Street Journal **www.wsj.com**
WebEx **www.webex.com**
Yahoo! **www.yahoo.com**

Chapter 9

Keeping Up with Technology

In his book, *Data Smog: Surviving the Information Glut* (Harper San Francisco, 1998), author David Shenk looks at the flood of information that bombards us every day. Some of that smog surely is the jargon, specifications, and instructions that accompany new developments in information technology. How do you wade through everything you have to learn and keep up with constantly evolving Internet technology while running a business?

One key is to conscientiously spend part of every day online. This requires commitment but not necessarily a lot of time. Beyond that, here are eight other strategies for keeping current:

Think in Internet time. "It's important to learn to think in Internet time," says Buzz Reid, vice-president of strategic planning for Golfballs.com, a 25-employee retailer/wholesaler of golf balls, based in New Iberia, La. "The Internet has caused our business to increase faster than any other business any of us has ever been involved with. We've been growing 300% to more than 500% for the past several years," says Reid, who explains that the dramatic growth has come about for a number of reasons. Golfballs.com, exists almost exclusively on the Internet. Being on the Internet has encouraged managers to think outside the box and look for marketing techniques that a normal bricks-and-mortar retailer might not consider. The company identified a need that could be satisfied by Internet marketing: Many countries have few golf balls available; others have golf seasons that occur in different months than those in the United States. Result: an instant global market.

Look ahead. "Internet time is like a dog's life," observes Reid. "One year is equal to seven. You can't plan where a normal business might be in a year or two because you will be there in six to nine months or less, and it may take two to six months to implement your plan. Scalability with networking technology is where you have to concentrate, or be left behind."

For example, says Reid, suppose you need to implement an accounting software package throughout your company. If you select a package based on your current needs and don't plan ahead, you might spend as much as $2,500 for implementation and conversion but outgrow the software in the three to six months it takes for installation. In contrast, a package that gives you some scalability may cost $25,000 or more, but you'll have more time to install and use the software before you have to implement another new product.

Communicate more quickly. As a manager you should always look for new ways to communicate faster and more efficiently. The fastest growing area in Internet communications is in mobile connectivity. Cellular phones, palm devices, and handheld appliances that can surf the Web are proliferating so that developers are having difficulty creating special small-format versions of Web sites so that users can view those sites on miniature screens.

Monitor your software. When you use Internet technology to run your internal network and do business online, you have to keep up with upgrades for the following types of software:

> **TIP** Applications such as Adobe Photoshop (about $600 per user) or Microsoft Word ($250 when purchased with Microsoft Office 2000) can be expensive, especially if you need to purchase more memory for each machine that runs the software, and if you need to purchase updates for all staff members who plan to use the product. One way of getting around the constant updating routine is to "rent" the programs from an application service provider (ASP). You don't have to own your own copy of the program; you lease it from the ASP and then use it online.

TIP If you're considering one of the new portable-access devices, try before you buy. At this writing, their Internet connection speeds are only 9.2Kbps to 14.4Kbps, which is far slower than the fastest dial-up speed of 56Kbps. Although the NeoPoint 1000, for example, can display 11 lines of text, other phones that can surf the Web show even less detail. In order for Web sites to display data on the tiny screens of portable-access devices with their slow Internet connections, the sites must pare down their displays (text only or limited graphics).

A standard protocol, called wireless application protocol (WAP), has emerged to handle wireless data. A WAP-compatible Web site can format and transmit data specifically for wireless devices regardless of the type of device or the service provider. However, at this writing only a fraction of Web sites are WAP compatible, so the number of sites that can be viewed optimally on a handheld or cell phone screen is limited.

If you plan to access the Net or check e-mail frequently with a portable-access device, avoid access plans that give you 20 to 30 hours per month for a set fee (usually from $19.99 to $59.99) but charge premium fees (35¢ per minute in some cases) if you exceed the time limit. Instead, look for all-in-one pricing plans.

- *Server software.* Programs, such as Microsoft Internet Information Server, that make files available on your local network
- *Operating systems.* Programs, such as Windows NT 4.0, that enable individual users to work with files on their own computers and share them
- *Applications.* Programs such as word processing, spreadsheet, and others used to perform specific business tasks

How do you know when it's time to switch from, say, Microsoft's Windows NT to Windows 2000 for running the computers on your network? Pay attention to Web sites that review such software and explain the new features in a nutshell, such as CNET or ZDNet.

Monitor network speed and reliability. It's important to ensure that your network has adequate computing power to handle the traffic. Depending on the size of your company you might need groups of servers, called server clusters, to handle the increase in data. (This is referred to by tech types as *load balancing*.)

If you expect to work with particular computing experts, such as Internet service providers (ISPs), network consultants, and maintenance companies, you may want to establish service-level agreements that define the amount of service you expect to receive. Such agreements can be crafted to help ensure that you will continue to receive adequate service, even if your equipment fails.

Check industry news sources. Obviously, you can't read all the Internet-related magazines and Web sites that vie for your attention, but you can choose one or two good sources and follow them regularly. CEOs on the 1999 *Inc.* 500 list of the nation's fastest-growing small businesses say they consult the following news sources most frequently:

• Search engine: Yahoo!
• News source: CNN
• Business information source: *The Wall Street Journal*

It's a good idea to subscribe to a few

> **TIP** You can choose which news you want to view by downloading Personal Notifier software, developed by Lycos, that lets you select the type of news stories and items (e.g., names of individual stocks) you want to track each day.

> **TIP** Where do you find a mailing list for your field of business? Go to Liszt, a collection of more than 90,000 mailing lists around the world, or consult trade magazines in your field. Many of these specialized publications run their own discussion groups and mailing lists. Or start your own affordable mailing list at SKYLIST.net: A list of 251 to 500 messages a month costs $250 to set up and $100 a month thereafter.

specialty magazines devoted to technologies that you use, such as *Extranet Strategist,* a news magazine devoted to the creation of, and security involved in, working with extranets.

Delegate to your staff. One of the best ways to stay afloat amid a flood of information is to have staffers filter it down to only what you need to know. Graham Weihmiller, founder and CEO of Manhattan-based DormNow.com, an e-commerce company that sells furnishings to college students through the Web site TheDormStore.com, came up with an innovative solution for staying informed about changes in the Internet marketplace.

Weihmiller outsources information gathering to a network of potential hires, friends, and other contacts that he calls shadow employees. When he finds someone he likes but can't yet hire, he'll tap that person for quick research projects such as collecting background information on a possible competitor. A side benefit is that both the company and the job candidate get to know each other better. "It brings them up the curve, so when we're ready to bring them on, they'll know exactly what's going on," he says.

Stay current by networking. You can do effective B2B marketing by talking to your peers in chat rooms or on mailing lists. Mailing lists are an especially good forum because you are likely to meet professionals in your field.

Esther Dyson, the well-known technology observer and editor of the newsletter *Release 1.0*, told *Inc.* magazine that she gets most of her information from e-mail and mailing lists. The lists are good, she says, "because there's someone out there filtering things for you and culling the best."

Bill Cameta, the owner of Cameta Camera, a photographic equipment retailer and film processor in Amityville, N.Y., allocates every morning to responding personally to e-mail inquiries. While you may not be able to spare an entire morning every week to clean out your e-mail inbox, it's a good idea to schedule an hour a day (perhaps half an hour in the morning and half an hour in the afternoon) to field e-mail and other inquiries.

The connections you can make with business peers—and what you can learn from them—are among the many benefits you can reap from using the Internet to run your business. ■

COMPANIES AND SITES IN THIS CHAPTER

Adobe Systems **www.adobe.com**
Cable News Network **www.cnn.com**
Cameta Camera **www.cameta.com**
CNET Networks **www.cnet.com**
DormNow.com **www.dormstore.com**
Extranet Strategist **www.extranet-strategist.com**
Golfballs.com **www.golfballs.com**
Inc. magazine **www.inc.com**
Liszt **www.liszt.com**
Lycos **www.lycos.com**
Microsoft **www.microsoft.com**
SKYLIST.net **www.skylist.net**
The Wall Street Journal **www.wsj.com**
Yahoo! **www.yahoo.com**
ZDNet **www.zdnet.com**

CyberSpeak

Algorithm A mathematical formula commonly used in computer programming to encrypt information sent from one computer to another over the Internet.

Application service provider (ASP) An Internet-based service that provides software or services that businesses can rent and use online through their Web browsers.

Authentication The process of identifying a user as an individual who is authorized to access information. In terms of Web security, authentication commonly takes the form of a user name and password that a user must provide to enter part of a Web site.

Back end (back office) Computer functions that a business or other service provider conducts that are invisible to the customer or end user, such as credit-card processing, shipping instructions, inventory management, and accounting.

Bulletin board Internet communications technology that enables groups of users to post messages on a page where they can be read and responded to by other users.

Chat Real-time discussions among Internet users who type messages to one another and view the resulting text on their computer screens.

Digital certificate A digital file that is issued by a certification authority (CA) and that establishes the identity of an individual or organization. A certificate contains the holder's name; a serial number; expiration dates; and a copy of the certificate holder's public key, which is a code used to exchange encrypted communications.

Digital subscriber line (DSL) A technology that uses conventional analog telephone lines to transfer digital data at high speeds over the Internet.

Discussion group Internet-based technology that brings together groups of users who share an interest. Users access and post messages using discussion-group software, which is built into Netscape Communicator and Microsoft Internet Explorer. Discussions are organized by topics called threads.

Encryption The process of transforming digital information from a readable to an unreadable format (and vice versa) by processing it with an algorithm.

Ethernet A high-speed networking technology that enables computers on a local area network (LAN) to exchange data at 10 Mbps or 100 Mbps (Fast Ethernet).

Extranet An area of a company's internal intranet that is made available to preferred customers, employees, or visitors who enter an approved user name and password.

CyberSpeak

Firewall Hardware or software that is placed on the periphery of an organization's network. All traffic going into the internal network from the Internet is screened by the firewall to prevent any unauthorized users from entering or accessing protected information.

Flame An abusive, often profane message sent from one Internet user to another in a discussion-group message or by e-mail.

Frame relay Technology that enables transmission of digital data at high speeds between local area networks or between end points in a wide area network (WAN). Data is transferred in a variable-size unit called a frame.

FrontPage server extensions Special software that is installed on a Web server in order to give added functionality to Web sites created with FrontPage 2000, such as the ability to process data submitted from Web-page forms or discussion-group pages.

Gigabit Ethernet A relatively new variation on the Ethernet local area network technology that permits rapid data transfer rates of one gigabyte per second.

Instant messaging (IM) Technology that allows users to send typed messages to each other in real time, while both are online. In order to communicate, users must have the same IM software, such as ICQ or AOL Instant Messenger.

Internet protocol (IP) A set of standard procedures that enables information to be transmitted from one computer to another on the Internet.

Internet service provider (ISP) A company that enables users to connect to the Internet. Users dial up one of the ISP's computers using a modem, or they are directly connected by DSL or a high-speed cable modem.

Intranet A local area network that uses Internet technology. Computers running Web-server software make files available to employees who use a Web browser file transfer protocol (FTP) program, or other Internet client software on their desktop computers to access shared data.

IP address A unique identifier for a computer on a network that consists of four sets of numbers separated by dots, such as 128.133.47.1.

Key A series of characters and/or numerals used to produce encrypted text. The longer the key, the more difficult it is to decrypt the text.

CyberSpeak

Mailing list An Internet-based communications forum that enables a group of individuals to conduct discussions by submitting e-mail messages to all the other members of the list. To join a list, users must subscribe.

Newsgroup See *Discussion group*.

Personal digital assistant (PDA) A catch-all designation that describes any handheld device that can perform computing functions or store digital information.

Portal A Web page visitors use to find information. The home pages of sites such as Yahoo! function as portals, leading users to specific areas of the Internet.

Public-key encryption A security scheme in which complex formulas, called private and public keys, are exchanged in order to send and receive encoded messages.

Secure sockets layer (SSL) A set of Internet security schemes used to encrypt and then decrypt transmissions between computers on a network.

Sound card A hardware device that plugs into a receptacle within a computer, called a slot, that enables the machine to play audio.

T1 line A high-speed, broad-bandwidth telephone line that can handle 1.544 Mbps of text or images or 24 voice channels; commonly used to connect to the Internet.

Thread Series of discussion group messages posted on a single topic.

Usenet An extensive part of the Internet that consists of thousands of public discussion groups called newsgroups.

Vertical community A community of Internet users that share a particular field of interest, whether personal or business-related.

Videoconferencing Technology that enables face-to-face meetings with audio on users' networked computers.

Virtual workgroup A group of computer users who collaborate on projects by e-mail, conferencing, or other Internet technologies.

Virus A potentially harmful computer program that can damage software or hardware and that is often designed to be spread to other computer users.

Voice-over Internet protocol (VoIP) The transmission of voice communications over the Internet through Internet protocol (IP).

About the Author

Greg Holden is president of Stylus Media, a Chicago-based group of editorial, design, and computer professionals who produce print and electronic publications. A freelance business writer as well, he has written 12 books, including *Starting an Online Business for Dummies, Small Business Internet for Dummies,* and *Creating Web Pages for Kids and Parents* (all published by IDG Books Worldwide). His newest book, *Literary Chicago: A Book Lover's Guide to the Windy City* (Lake Claremont Press), was published in fall 2000.

Holden, who earned a M.A. in English from the University of Illinois at Chicago, also writes a biweekly column, "E-business Insider," for the online new media service CNET; a monthly column, "E-Commerce Makeover," for the online magazine ComputerUser.com; and regular articles on Internet business topics for *Publish* magazine.

Acknowledgment: **David Talbott**, of the virtual literary agency StudioB, served as the liaison between *Inc.* Business Resources and Greg Holden, author of this book. StudioB (www.studiob.com) matches authors with businesses and organizations that need writing and material that focuses on technical subjects in non-technical language.